Grist for the Mill

Grist for the Mill

Awakening to Oneness

Ram Dass with Stephen Levine
Revised Edition

HarperOne
An Imprint of HarperCollins Publishers

HarperOne

HarperCollins books may be purchased for educational, business, or sales promotional use. For information, please e-mail the Special Markets Department at SPsales@harpercollins.com.

HarperCollins website: http://www.harpercollins.com

HarperCollins®, ®, and HarperOne™
are trademarks of HarperCollins Publishers

REVISED EDITION

Library of Congress Cataloging-in-Publication Data
is available upon request.

ISBN 978-0-06-223591-6

23 24 25 26 27 LBC 24 23 22 21 20

The Dharma belongs to no one. Teachings about the Dharma come now through one person and now through another. What is contained in this book certainly did not originate with me. It is part of a river that flows through me from my Guru, teachers, parents, past incarnations, and life experiences.

As I read this manuscript, I can feel in the turn of a phrase or an image the intimate presence of my Guru and one or another of my teachers. Their very real contributions to this book are warmly and gratefully acknowledged. May this book serve as an expression of appreciation for their teachings.

My thanks also to Stephen Levine, co-author, whose sensitive, poetic collaboration made the words come to light as I heard them but could not quite speak them.

Shanti,

Ram Dass

New York City, 1976

Contents

Introduction

Grist for the Mill came from talks I gave to different groups in the 1970s. It captures those interchanges, but it's also about living in the moment, which transcends time. Stephen Levine and I thought these talks would have broad appeal.

The spiritual path is an inner exploration. It exists for anyone at any time who looks within to examine the premise of their own identity or to seek the transcendent reality of the universe. Consciousness is a shared quality of human existence. Except for those rare saintly beings who take birth solely for the benefit of humanity, to teach and inspire, most of us turning on this wheel of birth and death suffer similar afflictions of mind and seductions of the senses.

The astonishing diversity of human nature and individual karma means everyone has their own particular spiritual path and methods that work best for them. *Grist for the Mill* goes from a general map of the terrain of the spiritual path to answering people's specific questions.

The primary method we explore uses whatever comes to you in life as food for your spiritual path. At the time I wrote *Grist for the Mill,* my practice was to see everything that came my way as a manifestation of the Divine Mother who is the energy, or Shakti, of all creation. Around this time I studied with a female teacher named Joya, who for a while represented Shakti for me. I give a chronicle of the ups and downs of that trip here as well.

We Westerners are enthralled with our minds, and I am no exception. I am often the best object lesson for my own teaching. Strategies in the book involve ways to use the mind to go beyond the mind, ways to understand states of consciousness that are beyond thought, and ways to identify ourselves other than through our mind, through our intuition, and so forth. Included are Buddhist ideas about non-self, and how to witness the mind and our attachment to it. Another approach we explore is devotion, or bhakti, in which everything is seen through the lens of love for the Divine.

To understand the sometimes gradual nature of the path, I find it helpful to conceive of a spiritual journey that goes beyond this lifetime. In that view the time factor for souls is an infinity of multiple incarnations, though paradoxically reality lies in being fully present in each moment.

Paradoxes like the infinity of time vs. the timeless present, self vs. non-self, and the need for individual effort vs. surrender to a higher power are all grist for the mill of treading on this pathless path. My Guru, Maharaj-ji, once told me, "Enjoy everything!" These days I try to simply love everything that comes my way, whether animate or inanimate, pleasant or painful. I hope you too can learn to absorb life's ecstasies and distresses into your spiritual practice so they are just more grist for the mill.

Namaste,
Ram Dass
Maui, 11 June 2012

Collaborator's Note

The space from which these understandings come has no body, no mouth, it cannot speak. To be communicated, these insights had to cross the wild river of accumulated personality, acculturation, interpretation, opinion, and preference to enter into the limitations of language. They are offered as a near translation of the experience of things as they really are. These teachings were originally offered in the direct, charismatic, air medium of the oral tradition before once again being translated and further grounded into the powerful earth medium of the written word, print on paper, book form.

The transmission from form to form continued without the self-conscious "presence" of an editor, but instead flowed from the experience out of which these teachings had originated. The continuity was grace elicited from the fullness of each moment as it manifested before us as this book. The collaboration occurred on a plane where the beings collaborating were no one in particular, so there was little to impede or diffuse the natural intensity of the light.

As this oral tradition translated itself into the written word, we decided not to italicize, specialize, the Sanskrit-derived terms such as: sadhana, spiritual practice; karma, the actions of life which breed further reaction; samadhi, deeply concentrated states; Guru, the teacher, the teaching—because these concepts should not be something different, or "other," but should be allowed to enter into the marrow of the language. So too dharma, as natural karmic duty, appropriate action for this incarnation, is not capitalized for it is "nothing special," while Dharma, as the truth, Natural Law, the Tao, God's will, is capitalized to demonstrate its profound universality.

Interwoven from lectures, retreats, articles, and interviews given during 1974–1976 in Philadelphia, Washington, Lincoln, Seattle, Los Angeles, Boston, Portland, San Francisco, Santa Cruz, Kansas City, and Aspen, and updated for current readers, these words are offered as the gift of the Dharma, which is ever and always present to each of us, in each of us.

Let it shine,
Stephen Levine
Santa Cruz, 1976

Preface to the Previous Edition

In the first half of the seventies, spiritual growth rooted in Eastern mysticism was definitely "in." There was a proliferation of spiritual teachers (often self-proclaimed gurus) with sizeable followings. This movement coincided with the psychological growth movement, another significant flowering of that period. Cynics among us referred to these turnings inward as a reflection of narcissism and dubbed the participants the "me generation." But it was not just narcissism. In part, these movements represented a healthy balancing after the blood-letting polarization in political action that occurred in our society at the time of the Vietnam conflict.

Though the spiritual groups were often quite flamboyant and smacked of what Trungpa Rinpoche—a Tibetan Lama—referred to as "spiritual materialism," at their root was a genuine yearning to connect with a deeper context from which to lead a life of greater consciousness and equanimity. It was in response to this yearning that this book originally appeared in the mid-seventies.

For the most part, this book is an edited transcript of words spoken at various gatherings during that period. In lecturing, I do not usually follow formally prepared material. Rather, through meditation I empty my mind before speaking, in order that my words might speak from and to those places in the audience and in myself which require that we say again what must still be heard at that moment on our journey.

Now, years later, as I reread this material on the occasion of its republication, I am surprised at how timely the message seems . . . or perhaps I should say, how outside of time. Perhaps what we need to hear now, just as we needed to hear then, are those eternal verities that Aldous Huxley refers to as the "Perennial Philosophy," the message which, through form after form, comes down relatively unchanged through the ages. In these days of planned obsolescence, when the shelf-life of new books is measured in days, I find the unchanging nature of these ideas reassuring.

At the same time, I found expressions and metaphors, as well as political or social references, that dated the material. In cases where I felt that the expressions or referents would not be understandable to today's reader, I have changed and updated them. And in the cases where I feel that my attitudes and understanding toward some issues have matured over these years, I have also adapted the material.

In the sixties, when we first encountered Eastern ideas of enlightenment, we expected to be personally enlightened in a matter of a year, or a decade at the most. This attitude was slightly tempered in the seventies, but still we expected enlightenment during this lifetime. But now, we have come to appreciate the fine print in the Eastern texts, and that, along with our own experiences, has helped us become free of applying temporal achievement criteria to our spiritual work. We have learned patience and humility and an understanding that we practice dharma without attachment to the goal . . . simply because it is the obvious thing to do. So in places where my presentation seemed immaturely and unnecessarily arrogant, I have softened the material.

Since this book first appeared, there have been periods when material acquisition and personal pleasure have taken priority over spiritual aspirations. For example, the great interest in Eastern philosophy on college campuses for a time gave way to a marked increase in pragmatic career choices with the promise of high financial reward. Many of the deeper personal and social values reflected in the sixties and the seventies seemed to have disappeared into the background. Now, once again, the pendulum swings. In high schools and colleges, there is evidence of a new social concern for the suffering of others, and there is once again an upswing in interest in inner growth. As my friend Wavy Gravy has said, "The eighties are the sixties twenty years later." Now with the sixties a half-century in our rear-view mirror, the Perennial Philosophy is once again coming into flower in our culture. I hope that books such as this one, in its new incarnation, can help to cultivate that process.

Ram Dass
Cohasset, Massachusetts, 1987

In India when we meet and part we often say, "Namasté," which means: I honor the place in you where the entire universe resides; I honor the place in you of love, of light, of truth, of peace. I honor the place within you where, if you are in that place in you, and I am in that place in me, there is only one of us.

Namasté

Chapter 1

The Journey

Welcome! It's so graceful to share the journey. We've been on this journey a long time together. We've gone through a lot of stages. And just as in any journey, some people have dropped along the way, have had enough for this round. Others have been waiting for us to catch up. The journey passes through the seven valleys, the seven kingdoms, the chakras, the planes of consciousness, the degrees of faith. Often we only know we've been in a certain place when we pass beyond it, because when we're in it, we don't have the perspective to know, because we're only being. But as the journey progresses, less and less do you need to know. When the faith is strong enough, it is sufficient just to be. It's a journey toward simplicity, toward quietness, toward a kind of joy that is not in time. It's a journey out of time, leaving behind every model we have had of who we think we are. It involves a transformation of our being so that our thinking mind becomes our servant rather than our master. It's a journey that takes us from primary identification with our body, through identification with our psyche, on to an identification with our soul, then to an identification with God, and ultimately beyond identification.

Because many of us have traversed this path without maps, thinking that it was unique to us because of the peculiar way in which we were traveling, often there has been a lot of confusion. We have imagined that the end was reached when it was merely the first mountain peak—which yet hid all of the higher mountains in the distance. Many of us got enamored because these experiences along the way were so intense that we couldn't imagine anything beyond them. Isn't it a wonderful journey that at every stage we can't imagine anything beyond it? Every point we reach is so much beyond anything up until then that our perception is full and we can't see anything else but the experience itself.

For the first few stages, we really think that we planned the trip, packed the provisions, set out ourselves, and are the master of our domain. Only after traversing a few valleys and mountains along the way do we begin to realize that there are silent guides, that what has seemed random and chaotic might actually have a pattern. It's very hard for a being who is totally attached and identified with his intellect to imagine that the universe could be so perfectly designed that every act, every experience is perfectly within the lawful harmony of the universe—including all of the paradoxes. The statement, "Not a leaf turns but that God is behind it," is just too far out to think about. But eventually we begin to recognize that the journey may be stretching out for a longer span than we thought it was going to.

We come out of a philosophical materialistic framework in which we are totally identified with our bodies and the material plane of existence—when you're dead, you're dead—so get it while it's hot. And more is better and now is best, because we don't know when the curtain will come down and it will all be over. And better not to think about that curtain because it's too frightening. Where along the journey do we begin to suspect that that model of how it is, is just another model? And that this lifetime is but another part of a long, long journey? In the Buddhist teachings, there is an analogy of how long we've been doing this. The image is that of a solid granite mountain six miles long, six miles wide, six miles high. Every hundred years a bird flies by the mountain with a silk scarf in its beak and runs the scarf over the mountain. In the length of time it takes for the silk scarf to wear away the mountain, that's how long we've been doing it. Round after round after round. It puts a different time perspective on this one life, doesn't it? Not all of those rounds are on this plane; not all of those rounds are in human form. But all of those rounds are a part of a journey that has direction.

Sooner or later the realization comes that nothing we can think of is going to do it. Nothing we experience is it—because our minds think of things, and we and the things are separate, and there is a little veil, like a trillionth of a second that exists between us and the thing we're thinking of. And when we sense something or collect an experience, there's the distinction between the experience and the experiencer, and that's a very thin veil. It doesn't matter how thin it is—it's like steel. It always separates us from where it's happening.

When at last the despair is deep enough, we cry out. We cry inwardly or outwardly, "Get me out of this! I want to get out! I give up. I don't know. I surrender." At that moment, when the despair is genuine enough, the veil separates a bit. I'm not talking about wanting to want to give up. I'm not even talking about wanting to give up. I'm talking about actually giving up. The problem is, most of us say, "I don't think my thoughts are going to do it, so I'm now open to new possibilities. I'll read Ram Dass's book, but I'm going to sit and judge it." Forget it—because the judge has designed the game so that the judge won't have to change, and says, "Anything that doesn't fit in with the way I thought it was, I reject." We have categories for that—it's "weird" or it's "occult" or it's "far out" or whatever we want to call it. It's a way of putting it somewhere else so it doesn't blow our scene up. That's what the judge's function is, so the scene doesn't get blown up.

When, as the Third Chinese Patriarch of zen suggests, we set aside opinion and judgment because we see they're just digging us deeper into our hole, we surrender our own knowing. Now, that's really hard, because the whole culture is based on the worship of the golden calf of the rational mind while other levels of knowing, like what we call intuition, have practically become dirty words in our culture. It's sort of sloppy, it's not tight, logical, analytic, clean. You don't sit in scientific meetings and say, "I intuit that . . ." You say, "Out of inductive reasoning, I hypothesize that we will be able to disprove the null hypothesis." That's saying the same thing, but we've made believe that we're doing it analytically and logically. Some of us, I am sure, recognize that game. When Einstein said, "I did not arrive at my understanding of the fundamental laws of the universe through my rational mind," many of his colleagues thought him quite eccentric—because the rational mind has been the high priest of the society. Realize that it's merely a tiny system and that there are meta-systems and meta-meta-systems, in which only when we transcend our logical analytic mind can we even enter the gate.

I remember as a social scientist, I studied what was studiable. What was studiable had nothing to do with what was happening to me, but it was studiable. The analogy is the drunk looking for the watch under the streetlight. Someone comes to help him look, but there's no watch under the streetlight, and finally the passerby asks, "Well, exactly where did you lose it?" And the drunk says, "I lost it up in the dark alley, but there is more light out here." It is the light of the analytic mind we were using to try to find what had been lost in the distant alley.

Well, a long time ago we were enamored of our prehensile capabilities, the fact that our thumb and index finger could do intricate stuff that no other species could. That was pretty far out; we got a lot of power. But that was nothing like all the anticipatory stuff and the remembering and all this stuff we could do with our cerebral cortex. And to think that wasn't to be the end-all. It even sent people to the moon. Isn't that the ultimate? It doesn't seem to be, does it? It's interesting that people were burned at the stake for suggesting that the anthropomorphic view of the universe wasn't the final one. We all have been caught again and again in embracing the view that the physical universe is the center of it all, when in fact it turns out that the physical universe is just another universe. Not even necessarily the most interesting one. Isn't that damaging to our ego?

And the moment when there is that little bit of giving up, whether we're blown out of our rational mind by whatever techniques we have available, or some traumatic experience happens that shakes us out of it, or we have just lived long enough that we've despaired of ever getting it the way we thought we were going to—whatever the genesis of it, at that moment we experience the presence of another set of possibilities of who we are and what it's all about. It is like that moment depicted on the ceiling of the Sistine Chapel when the hands of God and man are just about to touch. It's just at the moment when the despair is greatest, when we reach up, that the grace descends, and we experience the knowledge or the insight or the remembrance that it all isn't in fact the way we thought it was. If it happens too violently, we decide we've gone insane.

And there are people who are all too willing to reassure us that we have, and there are places for that. In hunting tribes, mystics are treated as insane—they're an inconvenience because the tribe has to be kept mobile, and old people and crazy people have to be put away somewhere. But if we're in a certain position at the moment of seeing through, if the view has been gentle or if we're with somebody else who knows, or if we had intellectually known but didn't believe, all of which is a karmic matter, if we had some kind of structure or support system, we say, "Even though everybody else thinks I'm mad, I'm not."

It's like when I was being thrown out of Harvard. There was a press conference, and all the reporters and photographers were interviewing me because I was the first professor to be fired from Harvard in a very long time. They all were looking at me as the fighter who had just lost the big fight. Here I was, a good boy who had built his career and finally reached Harvard and now was obviously going to disappear into ignominy. The major teaching institution had dismissed me in disgrace. They had that look on their faces you have when you're around a loser. And here I was every few days taking acid with my partner, Timothy, and my friends were going into these realms beyond realms beyond realms, and I was looking at the reporters and photographers as "those poor fellows." And I looked around and saw that everybody believed in only one reality to this situation except me; and I remembered, since I'm a clinical psychologist, that that was a definition of insanity. One of me was saying, "Boy, are you crazy." And the other was saying, "Go, go, go, you're right on!"

The moment at which we look up, the moment at which we look in, starts the journey back. The journey has gone from the One into the incredible paranoid multiplicity of this high technological materialistic structure. Then, when the despair is great enough, there is the turnaround, and we start to go back to the One. And at that moment, who we are starts to change—because up until then, we have been worshipping our individual differences—"I'm more beautiful, I'm younger, I'm smarter, or I wish I were"—or totally preoccupied with getting an individual difference that we could accentuate, because that's where the payoff was.

So we dress in silver sequins with golden blups, and that makes us special, and everybody says, "You're special." But then when we look around, and we get a sense of another reality, an awareness of presence—a place within us starts to draw us as inevitably and irrevocably as a flame draws a moth. For a long time, maybe many, many lifetimes, we'll keep soaring in close and getting our wings singed.

Now, whether our wings are being singed, whether the fire purifies us or destroys us, depends on who we think we are, because the fire can only burn our stash of clinging. The fire doesn't burn itself. And in truth, we are the fire.

Chapter 2

Receiving the Transmission

To receive a spiritual transmission, it is not sufficient just to talk about it. Now we have to become it, for the transmission that we come to share is, in truth, not a conceptual one. What I know, I will share with you, but there is more, and for us to receive more than the words, we have to acknowledge who we truly are. Because if we come with the certainty that we already know and that what we have is enough, then though we will hear the words, we will not receive the transmission. If we transported this moment to a cave in the Himalayas that we had all spent months getting to, and we entered the cave after much purification and sat before a teacher, we would be ready to receive the transmission. Now it is a question of whether in this form—in the place we are right now—with such easy access to these words, whether the same space can be created, for by the time we got to the Himalayan cave, we would recognize that what we're seeking in the transmission has very little to do with time and space. It has very little to do with our body, with our personality. It was only when Don Juan had destroyed Castaneda's personal history that the transmission could occur.

When you sit in an auditorium and there is a speaker, or you read a book, you tune in a set of receiving devices—your ears, your eyes, and your conceptual analytic mind. But to receive this transmission requires much more than the mind. It requires a desire in us—to use this birth in order to become who, in truth, we are. It requires a desire to become free of the kinds of clinging and attachment that keep distorting and narrowing our vision. It requires that we truly desire to know what we are doing here, what our function is here on Earth. To say, "I want more than the reality of my senses and my thinking mind," requires that we take those moments every one of us has had in our life when we have been in tune with the Tao, with the harmony of the universe, with the flow—when for a moment we set aside our separateness, our self-consciousness, and became part of the process, in the same way as a tree or a brook or wheat is part of the process, and bring them into the foreground at this moment and make them figure so that they stand out and put the rest of the forms of our life into the background.

We had in those few moments the answer to every question our minds could create and all the food our souls needed. It's only that we didn't know it. So we gather to remind one another who we are. What we're looking for is who is looking; it's happening all around us, and we are what's happening. So that next time we sit waiting for something to begin, we realize that there is nothing that needs to begin, for the beginning, the middle, and the end are already who we are.

Actually what it is that I can share with you has no time and no space. It is not really East as opposed to West; it is not now as opposed to then. It isn't the sole domain of any organized religion. It is that which is universal to all that lives in the true spirit. Each time I go out on a speaking tour, there are a number of us for whom the introductory lecture is appropriate. Others of us here are ready for the intermediate course, the 101 series. Perhaps a few of us would like the advanced graduate seminar because we are ready to specialize; we're prepared to make a commitment in our life.

For those of us who want the advanced course, if while we are together we cultivate the quietness in ourselves, we may receive the transmission we seek. If we don't get lost in the words—for the words are like birds—they fly in from one horizon and fly out toward the other. For those of us with very active minds who'd like to know what's happening, I will provide words. And the active minds can chew on them, collect them, write them down, and save them until they turn yellow, until there is a readiness to sit quietly and open our hearts and quiet our minds. Because the predicament is that the transmission that we in truth yearn to receive is not one that the rational mind can fully grok, can fully grasp, can fully appreciate. All the rational mind can do is get to the point where it is pointing and it says, "It went thatta way!" But to have what we seek, we have to go beyond knowing and become it. It is a peculiar predicament, that this knowledge can only be known by transforming ourselves into the knowledge itself.

Chapter 3

Rules of the Game

The simple rules of this game are being honest with ourselves about where we're at, and learning to listen, to be able to hear how it all is. Meditation is a way of listening more and more deeply, so we hear from a more profound space, exactly how it is. To hear how it is, we must be open to it, thus the open heart.

We can take our lives exactly as they are in this moment; it is a fallacy to think that we're necessarily going to get closer to God by changing the form of our lives, by leaving so-and-so, or changing our jobs, or moving, or whatever . . . by giving up our stereos, or cutting off our hair, or growing our hair, or shaving our beards, or. . . . It isn't the form of the game; it's the nature of the being that fulfills the form. If I'm a lawyer, I can continue being a lawyer. I merely use being a lawyer as a way of coming to God.

It is a fallacy to think that any form of life is necessarily more spiritual than any other. Ashrams are often the heaviest, most neurotic, political settings I've ever been in. They can also be very beautiful spiritual spaces, but by definition, just because we're living in some place called an ashram or a monastery, doesn't mean we're getting closer to God.

For someone who has grown in evolution to the point that she or he understands that this precious birth is an opportunity to awaken, is an opportunity to know and perhaps to be God, all of life becomes an instrument for getting there: marriage, family, job, play, travel—all of it. We spiritualize our lives. When Krishna says in the *Bhagavad Gita* that you should do what you do, but offer the fruits of your actions to Me, he means that we should do it all in relationship to becoming enlightened. So when someone says to us, "Who are you?" the answer is not "I am a lawyer" or "I am a housewife." It's "I am a being going to God. I do law in order to provide right livelihood, to protect this temple and fulfill my responsibilities, in order to go to God. I am living with so-and-so, in such and such a situation, because that situation is the optimum for me to fulfill my karma and allow me to go to God." It's as simple as that.

We find our way through this incarnation; each of us has a different path through. No path is any better than any other path; they are just different. We must honor our own path. For some of us, we will feel like half a being until we form a connection with another half, and then we will be able to go to God. Others of us will go alone on our journey to God. It's not better or worse; it's just different. If we can get over the value judgments, we can listen to what it is we need to do without getting caught in all of the social pressures about marriage or non-marriage.

The true marriage is with God. The reason we form a conscious marriage on the physical plane with a partner is to do the work of coming to God together. That is the only reason for marrying when we are conscious. The only reason. If we marry for economics, if we marry for passion, if we marry for romantic love, if we marry for convenience, if we marry for sexual gratification, it will pass and there is suffering. The only marriage contract that works is what the original contract was—we enter into this contract in order to come to God, together. That's what a conscious marriage is about.

In fact, that is what everything we're doing is about. When we're ready, we flip the figure and background—what was figure becomes background, and what was background becomes figure. Our personal story becomes a spiritual journey, our ego-centric universe becomes a particle in an infinite field of light.

We look around, and we find we have a whole set of existing relationships. Some of them are not based on sharing the journey to God; they have other reasons, and the reasons fall away, and the relationships fall away, because they were what we call friends, and we outgrow our friends. They go on different paths than we do. That's reasonable. Other beings we are connected with, we can't outgrow: parents, children, relatives of one sort or another. We don't walk away. That is our given karma of the incarnation. We may grow at a different rate than they do, and they become the fire of our purification—because they will pull on us as we used to be, and our job is to deal with that until we get so even and clear that somebody can come up and say, "Hello, Dick," or "Hello, Richard," or whatever. And I'm right there. "Yes." Not, "I'm Ram Dass now." We work with the karma that exists in our life space.

Now, marriage is very peculiar in this situation because originally the marriage contract put our partners in the same relationship as a parent or child. It was not something we could walk away from, like a friendship. It was "until death do us part," and it became that kind of karma that we worked on. And even if our husband or our wife turned out to be the worst bastard or bitch in the world, that was our work! And if we really wanted to be with God, it didn't really matter. On the other hand, some of us may have gotten into the present cultural position of seeing marriages as special friendships, or even not so special anymore; people move in and out of them the same way they have friends—outgrow them and drop them. Now, in terms of the karmic situation, if we have married unconsciously, we are faced with an unconscious predicament, and whether we stay with our partner or not is not as gross a karmic matter, as if we had entered into the relationship consciously and then broken it off. That's a different matter.

It would be the same thing with abortion. Unconscious people who don't understand get abortions. And the karma is reasonably light because it comes out of the mechanicalness of mind in them. They're not aware of what they're doing. They're functioning totally in terms of lust and greed and fear and personal agendas of the mind and so on. They're just lost. But once a being has awakened and is aware of his or her predicament, then one style of life isn't that different from another. It's all grist for the mill. They don't sit around killing this and keeping that alive in order to make their lives nice. They take it as it comes down the pike and work with it.

There is no form that in and of itself is closer to God. All forms are just forms . . . not better to stay single than to marry, not better to marry than stay single. Each individual has his or her unique karmic predicament; each individual must therefore listen very carefully to hear her or his dharma or way or path. For one person it will be as a mother, or for another it will be to be Brahmacharya, or celibate. For one it will be to be a house-holder, for another to be a sadhu, a wandering monk. Not better or worse.

To live another's dharma, to try to be Buddha or to be Christ because Christ did it, doesn't get us there; it just makes us mimics. This game is much more subtle; we have to listen to hear what our trip through is, moment by moment, choice by choice. Is this one getting me closer or isn't it? And then we'll learn how truth gets us closer, how straightness gets us closer. We'll learn how simplicity of mind gets us closer. We'll learn how an open heart gets us closer. Certain acts—for example, like smoking pot—may show us the place, but over time they don't necessarily keep getting us closer. When we're finally really honest with our-selves about it, we recognize that it showed us a possibility, but it doesn't allow us to become the possibility. In fact we get to rec-ognize that happiness doesn't necessarily awaken us faster than sadness or unhappiness or pain or suffering—quite the reverse, it turns out. Pain and suffering awaken us more, because the only reason we experience pain or suffering is because we are clinging to something or other.

When we have the compassion that comes from understand-ing how it is, we don't lay a trip on anybody else as to how they ought to be. We don't say to our parents, "Why don't you under-stand about the spirit and why I'm a vegetarian?" We don't say to our husband or wife, "Why do you still want sex when all I want to do is read the *Gospel of Ramakrishna*?" A conscious being does all that he or she can to create a space for being with God but does no violence to the existing karma to do it. So we work with our fire, but not patronizingly, because we're not superior; we're just different. We understand about incarnation and that surrounding us are beings at every level of incarnation—some of them very new beings who just started to take human forms and are very busy materially getting it together, and other beings who are very old, who have been born again and again and again, and they've worked out an incredible amount of karma and are all ready to float into the akasha, to float back into God.

Some of the beings around us every day are very ancient beings, and some are very new. But is it better or worse? It's just different. Is it better to be twenty years old than fifty? It's just different. Do we judge someone because he or she's not as conscious as we are? Do we judge a prepubescent because they're not sexually aware? We understand. We have compassion. Compassion, sometimes, is simply leaving other people alone. We don't lay trips. We exist as a statement of our own level of evolution. We are available to any human being, to provide what they need, to the extent that they ask. But we see that it is a fallacy to think that we can impose a trip on another person.

I used to meet people, and I'd visualize how they could be, and my desire to have them change made me look into their eyes and touch them in a certain way, and they'd start to be who I wanted them to be. Then I'd say, "Look at that," and they'd say, "Oh thank you, thank you." And they'd love me and want to follow me around. But the next day or week or month, they'd come down because they were living out my desire, not theirs. They were living out my concept of how they ought to be, not being how, in fact, they needed to be in their own journey of evolution. The best we can do is become an environment that allows every person we meet to open in the optimum way they can open. The way you "raise" a child is to create a space with your own love and consciousness to allow that child to become whatever he or she can become in this lifetime.

It's the same if we're therapists or marriage partners or spiritual teachers; whatever our roles in human relationships, the game is always the same. If you're a police officer on traffic duty, your job may be to give people traffic tickets. How you give those traffic tickets is a function of your evolution. You can give people traffic tickets in such a way that they'd end up enlightened—because there is no form to this game at all. It's who's in the form that counts. It isn't how holy we look; it's how much we *are* the spirit of the living Christ, the compassion of the Buddha, the love of Krishna, the fierce discriminating wisdom of Tara or Kali. There's no one action or emotion that's holier than any other. People get into thinking one form of emotional action is more holy. For example, Maharaj-ji said to me, "Ram Dass, give up anger." And I said, "Well, Maharaj-ji, can't I even use anger as a teaching device?" And he said *angrily,* "No!" There are many levels to this game; they sneak up on us.

Of course there are certain acts that conscious beings do not perform—not that they couldn't be performed consciously, but that it doesn't come into the flow. We are not able to hide behind form for long. Many people say to me, "Should I be a vegetarian or shouldn't I?" "Should I have sex or shouldn't I?" "Should I meditate forty minutes or shouldn't I?" People who meditate exactly the right number of minutes, eat exactly the right food, do all the things perfectly, can also be caught in the chain of gold, in the chain of righteousness and ritual. That is not liberation. But eventually one does perform the spiritual practices, not out of obligation, not out of guilt, but because we've got to do it. We demand it of ourselves. We end up going through hell in meditation to quiet our mind, not because somebody says, "You ought to quiet your mind," but because our agitated mind is driving us up the wall, and it's keeping us from getting on with it. We'll learn how to pray, and read holy books, and practice devotional acts and chants, opening our hearts and asking Christ to fill us with love, not because we're good, but because with a closed heart we know we cannot come into the flow of the universe.

Now, there are very delicate issues about passivity and activity and will and choice and so on. And we must listen very deeply within ourselves, for we are continually making choices, and the choices boil down to going either in the direction of the harmony and the flow and the will of God, the flow of the universe—or going against it. And we listen and feel that, with the deepest kind of honesty we've got. This journey is based on just two very simple concepts. Total honesty with ourselves, total honesty. If we make a mistake, admit it and get on with it. Don't cover errors. The whole spiritual journey is a continuous act of falling on our faces. And we get up and brush ourselves off and get on with it. If we were perfect, we wouldn't even go on a journey. We can't be afraid of making errors. We may choose the wrong teacher; we may get into a method that's no good. Many things can happen. We make errors; we correct them if we can, without hurting another being's spiritual opportunities. There is another rule for this game: we may never use one soul for another. If our journey to God is keeping another being from going to God, forget it. We're never going to get there. It's as simple as that. We have to listen to ourselves and be honest with ourselves. Those are the rules of the game. Listen inward and be honest. Now, when we listen inward, we may not even know what to listen to. There are dozens of voices saying, "Listen to me. I'm the one." "I'm the one, get all you can." See. "I'm the one. Give it all up." See. It's the superego and the id, and all these voices are vying to be center stage. And we keep listening for what the Quakers call the "still, small voice within." We listen deeper and quieter, deeper and quieter— the more we enter a meditative space, the clearer we hear our dharma, our flow, our way home, our route back to the source.

Chapter 4

The Evolutionary Cycle

Back in the sixties when we gathered, we were confused as to whether we were psychotic or spiritual. We needed to gather in order to reassure ourselves that if we were psychotic, at least there were a lot of us. We were freeing ourselves from a cultural model of a reality that had been considered absolute.

And as we started to break free, there was much melodrama: violence, anger, confusion, as well as bliss and delight. Some of the confusion came because we kept trying to make the outside different as a reflection of the fact that the inside was changing. Part of that was pure in the sense that the new inner being was manifesting a new outer being, and part of it was impure because our faith was still flickering and we needed new symbols in order to reassure ourselves that we were in fact different. Some may recall the period when men started to grow their hair long and the power of that symbol, along with communal statements and alternative economics. During the sixties we were confused between internal freedom and external freedom, between revolution and evolution, because we didn't have models in our heads that would allow us to appreciate the grandeur of the change that we were undergoing. So we kept reducing its implications and seeing it as a social, psychological, or political change.

During the late sixties and early seventies, there was a period of fanaticism in our spiritual involvement. We were importing models from the East at a great rate and trying very hard to convert ourselves but, consistent with our tradition of doing things from the outside in, although we were taking on a lot of the symbols and accoutrements and might have looked like Buddha from outside, on the inside we were just people who were trying to look like Buddha. We were very confused about vows and commitments, the relationship to teachers, the whole concept of Guru, and what the journey was about. In the sixties the word *God* was still taboo, so we talked about "altered states of consciousness."

Implicit in all that we were doing was still an attachment to the fact that *we* could do it, that who we were or who we thought we were could change ourselves and become whatever it was that Buddha was or Christ was. That is, we were living in a culture in which humans ruled nature, within obvious boundaries, and we were so addicted to the rational mind and its power that we assumed we could think our way out of any predicament, we could figure out a new way to be through our thoughts and through our doing. But the predicament is that enlightenment is not an achievement; enlightenment is a transformation of being. And the achiever goes as well as the achievement.

Most of us didn't bargain for the implications of the journey we found ourselves on. We started to understand that it might have something to do with what had been talked about as "God" or a "coming to God" or, if you would rather deal with the unmanifest, the state of Nirvana. And we didn't really want them—we wanted to want them. That's a different level of the game. For most of us, it has been quite enough to want to want God or to want to want enlightenment. That keeps us cool, safe, secure, with a feeling that we're moving in the right direction. It gets a little scary when you start to disappear into the Void. In *Be Here Now* we referred to it as "the crisp trip."

Our true strength lies in our honesty with ourselves about our predicament. We have tasted of something; we are drawn to it as a moth toward a flame. We recognize our own fear. There is less melodrama and dramatic histrionics, and we are patiently and consistently doing the purification of being that is necessary for this transformation to occur. We realize that we can't grab it—we tried that—nor can we ignore it—we all tried that. When we try to grab it, up we go and down we come, with nothing but another high to add to our collection of moldering butterflies. We try to push it away and go back to not remembering that there is something else, and we can't do that either. In the middle of our most intense sensual enjoyment—which we would like to get lost back into, there is always the voice that says, "You are now in the middle of your intense sensual enjoyment." We can't get in; we can't get out. And here we are.

The melodrama is passing away. We recognize now that we are bringing our external world genuinely and honestly into harmony with our inner perceptions, and we don't need to try so hard to create an external space to prove anything. We're learning not to overkill with our intellect, not to try to think our way into holiness, because it just ends up being another prison, and we get caught pretending we're something we're not.

We are developing a deeper philosophical understanding of the predicament we are in as mutants, as evolving beings. We're listening inside to see what it is that is keeping us from that place or space or realization or connection that we have touched, tasted, felt, or somehow known about, and we are starting to find the methods to get on with the work. We have begun to understand that, though we gather as a group and listen to one another, each of us is in a unique predicament, and that we must listen to our own hearts to hear what we need; we can't imitate anybody else's journey.

To characterize these individual differences in terms of evolution, let me share with you a model that is just a model. Imagine an evolutionary clock. At twelve o'clock there is perfect harmony, "the Tao" as the Chinese say, "the Way" Christ talks about. The perfect balance, the interrelationship of all things with nothing separate, each in its proper place. The tree is the perfect tree; the river is the perfect river; the human being is the perfect human being. All is in its perfection.

At one minute after twelve, something is separate. At twelve it was the Garden of Eden: perfect harmony and balance. Then came a bite of the apple, and suddenly they're wearing fig leaves, and God is asking, "Who told you that you were naked?" Where did shame come from? It came from self-consciousness. And where did self-consciousness come from? It came from identifying with our thinking mind and thus experiencing ourselves as separate from that which we think about. At 12:01 duality has been created: subject and object, thinker and that which is thought. Separateness.

From 12:01 to six, there is a continuous attempt to solidify, protect, and increase the power of our position as separate entities, to create security, gratification, power over the world around us, to re-create the feeling of well-being that existed when we weren't, but now we are. Who I am talking about is us; you understand what I'm saying?

Let's just imagine that twelve o'clock is a sort of total perfection; although it's obviously unlabelable, we'll call it "God," but since it really is unlabelable, maybe we better just call it "G-d" so we won't get confused. Now G-d has, within its perfection, the freedom for any entity, such as a human entity, to pit its will against the total will, or G-d's will. So at first there were beings pitting themselves against the system, against the harmony, then everybody was "us," and "them" was the forces of nature, the storms, and so on.

But between 12:01 and six o'clock, a bizarre thing happened. Slowly "them" started to become others of us. Our tribe was "us," and other tribes were "them." Then within the tribe there was the family, and pretty soon it was "our family" and everybody else was "them." And then, within the family, Uncle Dave screwed us on that business deal, so he was sort of "them." We couldn't really even trust the greater family that much; "us" had to be our immediate family. That's around four thirty or five o'clock. Then there was a generation gap—we can't trust elders or youth—so maybe "us" is just me and my wife or me and my husband. And then there's a sex difference, so I can't fully consider my spouse as "us," so then I'm "us" and everything else in the universe is "them." "I'm very strong. I've got my protection. I know where I am, see?" You think it would end there. But that's about 5:45. In the final fifteen minutes is what now is called the total alienation of an individual. From whom? From himself. So finally we're looking at ourselves from outside and we don't even trust ourselves, so we're "them" too.

And what was the greatest power we had to work with in this journey from twelve to six? What was the greatest siddhi, or power, that was available to us as long as we were attached to our senses and our thinking mind? It was our intellect. Look at what our intellect has done. Look at this illusion. Look at the awesome impact of technology. They are all extensions of the human mind. Suppose I'm living in Manhattan, where, except for Central Park, there isn't anything you see that hasn't been run through a human mind. It's living inside human intellect actually. And the power of the human intellect is based on discrimination, individual differences; if we can tell the difference between this and that, and we can do it better than anybody else, we get paid more. And this intellect, which now decided that it could do anything, started to create models of what it had to do in order to get into that space it remembered somewhere inside of itself as that perfect feeling of at-hOMe-ness, of perfect well-being. The intellect developed a number of strategies. The most obvious one in our culture is "more is better."

Most of us have been on that journey, haven't we? On the supersensual astral planes. "Have you heard that new record by the blups? Yeah, but have you heard it when you're in the bathtub—with somebody else? Have you heard it when you're in the bathtub with somebody else by candlelight? On a good stereo set? There's an incredible wine; put it at the side of the tub: musk oil in the bath, the incense, the candlelight, the wine, the other being, and the bath water is just right and on the stereo. . . . Oh. . . . Oh. . . ." More is better. The obvious predicament that the intellect has a difficult time with is the sneaking realization that more is never enough. Or, more is maybe enough for a moment, but it doesn't last.

If we watch the patterns of our desire system and mind, the end of our day goes something like: "I think I'll take a nap. Gee, I'd like a cup of tea. How about a cigarette with that? I'm gonna listen to that music. What are we gonna have for dinner? What do you want for dessert, ice cream? I'm gonna have some coffee. What's on television? No, let's go bowling. Bicycle? Great. Ice cream soda? Let's go home. Okay. Want to go to bed? Okay. Ah, that's great. Got a cigarette?" On and on and in the middle of the main course, we're already thinking about what we'll have for dessert. The way we deal with this game is by constantly keeping the things going by fast, like a sleight-of-hand trick. Knowing that none of them will last, we figure that enough of them with small enough spaces in between will keep the rush going. Rush after rush after rush. But it's like building a house on sand—and we can't stop, because it gets a little frightening if we stop. If those spaces in between get too big, there is depression, confusion, disorientation, anger, loneliness, self-pity, unworthiness. Such stuff! Yech! So keep it coming, Ma. More and more and more.

But it turns out that Christ was right when he said, "Lay not up your treasures where moth and rust doth corrupt and thieves break in." Buddha was right when he said, "The cause of suffering is craving," craving after things that are not permanent, and nothing is permanent. If we cling to anything in form, we're going to suffer. That was Buddha's point. What blue chip can we invest in, that we can stop feeling frightened about? Our bodies? Our bodies are decaying this very minute. Even the youngest person here is decaying. Fifty or sixty years from now, you know where your body will be, what it will look like? And your intellect? All the knowledge you've collected? Did you ever see a skull and consider what's been eaten away and who ate it? And do you know what that emptiness is? That's everything you think you know. No wonder we're frightened. If we're thinking that we're our thinking mind, or that we're our body, it's panic.

From twelve to six is the increasing hope that we can get it all together, get it to feel just right. But there's a scariness, because we're trying to do it in a dimension that exists in time, where everything changes, where we're going to lose everything. At the very least, we're going to die. As philosophical materialists—not materialists in gold Cadillacs but those who are attached to the senses and intellect, and what we can think about—we are afraid because when we're dead, we're dead. As we get close to dying, we start to get very frightened, and we start to push pretty hard. We say, "Doctor, you've got new pills; use them. Do anything. Save me. Freeze-dry me. Do anything. I don't want to die," and grab and hold the bedsheets and pay more and more and get more and more hysterical and get into intensive care units and keep alive even if they have to transplant everything. But no matter how hard we try, suddenly we're dead.

And then a voice says to us, "Hello." If we're philosophical materialists, this leads us to say, "I guess I didn't die." To which the voice replies, "Oh yes, you did." Just as an example, at one point Buddha with his clear vision looked back and saw his last ninety-nine thousand incarnations. And that was only some of them. Birth-death-rebirth-redeath, on and on. It's called the Wheel of Life [and Death].

Now, in the early period, say between twelve and three, every time we die, we're so caught in our own attachments to our senses and our mind, we're so deep in the illusion, that when somebody says we're dead, we deny it and stay in total confusion until we get sent into the next round. Which is all, as we will see, perfectly designed. Later, as we get on with this round of births and deaths, we realize our predicament. We are under the veil of illusion of the birth—we don't want to die; then we're dead, and we say, "Far out, there goes another one." At this point we look around, and we see all our old mothers and fathers and friends. "Oh, my, you were my wife this time. Last time you were my brother."

When we're more conscious, we share in the understanding of where we are situated on the clock, in the round of births and deaths. We begin to see exactly what the next birth has to do from a karmic point of view, what it has to work out. And when we design the next birth, we say, "Well, I think I should be born into the lower-middle class in New York City, and then around ten, I think I should get raped. That would be useful for that particular samskara, that deeply imbedded mental impression, that I've been working out from four thousand births back. Let's see. I'll have my first child when I'm eighteen," and on and on. We design it all the way through—up until how we'll die. When we've run it all through the computer, the right parents come together, the right combinations come up, and then comes the moment of birth. And there we go. We dive back down in.

Some beings enter into this trip at the moment of conception, others at the moment of birth. You can tell those babies who entered at the moment of birth—the baby comes into the world and has that kind of stoned-out look, like what the hell am I doing here? Like an old Lama who has been born, say, in the Bronx, and he would like to bless everybody, but he can't get it to work. The ones who entered in at the moment of conception are busy being babies already. "Waaaaaa, give me." Those who come in bliss, because the veil hasn't shut down yet, are most of the time around parents who are busy inside the veil saying, "You're a baby; you're a baby. Goo-goo, look at the little baby." Pretty soon you buy it, and there you are again. On and on and on and on. Until something interesting happens at six o'clock, or one minute past six. Up until then, in every birth we've gone back into the illusion that we are this body, we are this thinking mind, and we are these senses. Everything we think we could get is what we can sense and think about; we're grabbing, looking out and down, grabbing and grabbing and grabbing. And then suddenly at one birth there is a moment when the veil parts—albeit for just a second—and we stick our noses through, and we say, "Wow, it isn't how I thought it was at all." Maybe the veil parted for a millisecond, but that was all it took if we were ready.

The veil is parting all the time for everybody, but most of the time our karma is so heavy, and we're so used to the veil, that we're not ready, so the minute we do see through, we immediately deny it or push it away as hard as we can. Some years back, I read in the *New York Times* magazine an article on "Mysticism in America," which said that two-fifths of the population of the United States has had a genuine mystic transcendent experience, which means they saw through the veil. As I recall, though I can no longer find the article, in sampling that two-fifths of the population, 85 percent said, "It was the greatest experience of my life, but I never want to have it again." Of course not, because look at how it upsets the apple cart. If we've built a whole universe around being somebody, and suddenly we see that that isn't who we are at all, what then?

But what is the condition necessary so that the moment comes when we see through the veil in a way that changes everything from then on, so that from a minute past six to twelve o'clock our whole journey changes its meaning? What's necessary for that to happen is despair. We realize that everything we think we can do to create perfection isn't going to be enough, that who we are and who we think we are is where the problem lies. It leads to a deep despair that seems to be a necessary condition for us to awaken at that moment. Once we have seen and know we have seen, we can never totally go back to sleep again. Even though we may forget for moments—and we will go through many, many more births between six and twelve o'clock—we can never fully forget. We are starting to be drawn back to twelve o'clock.

I'm talking about a clock of births and deaths that is all in time, which is all an illusion or relatively real, but we're just working with this metaphor for a moment. The beings in tune with these words, by nature, are by definition after six o'clock. Otherwise there'd be no reason for you to have read this far. Maybe you're at 4:13, but why would you put up with this long rap when you could be out getting more, which is better? But you know something? You're trapped in what you know, and look at what it's led you to.

And it gets worse; that's what's so extraordinary about it: once we start at one minute past six, the return journey to twelve, we're trying to grab at experiences that are going to get us back. We're going to collect new experiences that are called "getting high."

We come down from something, and we treat that down as the time between the last time we got high and the next time when once again we'll get on with our journey to God or back to twelve or whatever we want to call it. As the experiential clock ticks on, we keep developing in our understanding of how it's all working, and we begin to recognize a peculiar phenomenon that, as C. S. Lewis points out, "You don't see the center of the universe because it's all center." We, in fact, are the center of a universe that has been designed perfectly in order to awaken us out of the illusion and that every experience we have is equally valid as grist for the mill of awakening. Our whole incarnation is the teaching.

Next we begin to realize that although they are all equal in teaching quality, some of our experiences seem to shake us more than others, that the model that we are stuck in, sometimes so subtly we don't even know it, is shaken by pain and suffering and all the negative qualities. At that point we recognize the bizarre phenomenon that suffering is grace. Now, that's heavy, because up until that time, we've been trying to optimize pleasure and minimize pain. When we realize that in its fullest dimension, we may still live to optimize pleasure and minimize pain, but whatever comes down the pike is all right. "Boy, am I depressed." Now, there's depression. Until finally "There's pleasure." "There's pain." "I just made a thousand dollars. Wow." Or, "Oh, I just got robbed." And the "Wow" and the "Oh" and the "Ah" and the "Uh," all of these alternatives are just more stuff—beautiful, delightful stuff. This incarnation is the absolutely optimal one that we must be in now in order to do what needs to be done, or have done through us what needs to be done, in order to bring us home, bring us hOMe, or out or in. It's happening whether we know it or not. But as we know it, it changes it. That's part of it. That's all karma too.

Along around ten or eleven, we're going into other planes of reality in our meditation, and they are equally as real as the plane that we started this incarnation in. We don't quite understand where we are. Sometimes we get confused. It's very uneven and complicated work. But if we're really aiming at perfected truth, we move at a rate at which we can keep it all perfectly together. We work for the perfect balance of the different planes. At one minute past six we started to awaken and got so fascinated with what we started to see, we couldn't take our eyes off it, and we forgot to look down and we fell on our faces. We started to study the "absolute truths of God" and got so fascinated with the impersonal perfection of the universe beyond all polarities, we were so involved in the icy-cold impersonality of it all that we kept stepping on things and said, "Well, so what? It's all perfect."

But we learn the simple rule of the game is that as long as we push away one plane to grab another, we're still off balance. Ultimately, we understand that the truth must be balanced with the caring, with honoring of this incarnation. That's when we start to develop the capacity to look up and to look down at the same moment. To look in and to look out.

When we look at pure truth, we can see the grace that suffering is. From our point of view, when we're suffering, "Fine, I'm suffering. That's interesting." At the same moment, if we are looking down and honoring our incarnation, we're working to alleviate suffering. Let me give you an example. Somebody says, "I want to study yoga with you. I want to fast." And you say, "All right, fast for nine days." At the end of the seventh day, she says,

"I've fasted for seven days." And you say, "Wonderful, wonderful. You've got two more days to go." Then you walk outside the building, and somebody comes up to you and says, "Hey, man, you got a quarter? I haven't eaten in seven days." You don't say, "Wonderful, wonderful, you have two more days to go." It's not an appropriate response, because for that being, suffering isn't grace; suffering is a drag.

When that discipline is developed to allow us to look up and look down simultaneously, we have the absolute clarity of the pure white snow on the Himalayan peaks, the exquisite clarity, the raw truth, the impersonal perfection which includes everything—privation, starvation, persecution in our cities, inequality, violence, as well as all the bliss and love and compassion and kindness—the entire mosaic. In the icy peaks of the Himalayas, we see the perfection of it all in the evolutionary journey of beings. And at the same moment, the caring part of us is like the bleeding heart of Jesus, and we look down and see the blood on the snow. We keep both of those in mind at every moment so we can help beings who are suffering in the way they need to be helped.

If we are really going to help them get out of the illusion, we ourselves must not get lost in the illusion. We must continue to keep our eyes fixed on absolutely clear truth. We love without clinging; we help without identifying ourselves as helpers; we protest without getting lost in our protests; we care for our children remembering that, behind it all, here we are: the truth, the caring. We honor our bodies; we honor our society; we honor our whole game; we change it in the way it needs to be changed. We listen to hear what our particular karmic predicaments are in this round, and we find our dharma, the way to live this life in perfect harmony with the forces inside and outside of us in order to bring us home.

If we get greedy and try to push or pull, we're going to fall on our faces. If we go up to sit in a cave, we'll become so holy that light will be pouring out of our heads, everybody will be falling at our feet, and we'll have great powers. But when we try coming into New York City, we will see that there are little seeds inside of us, as Ramakrishna talks about, that never quite got cooked. It's an interesting point of view when we say, "Hey, I can't stand to live in the city. I've got to live out in the country." What we're really saying is, "I can't stand those things in myself that the city fans." Believe me, if there's nothing that we want, the city is the same as the Himalayan peak. All the city is showing us is stuff in ourselves that we wish we didn't have.

As we get farther along in this journey, the pull of twelve o'clock gets so fierce and we want to get done so badly that we can taste it and, at that point, we say, "Give me the fire. I want a hot fire. Make it hotter, hotter. Come on, give it to me." Then, when somebody gets us furious, we know that the only reason we got angry was because we had a secret hidden model of how we think it ought to be that we were holding on to. We realize that the person who got us angry is a teaching, and in our minds we thank him. We get so eager to root out the stuff in us that's keeping us from getting on, from awakening, that we start to look for situations to force us to do it.

Once, I spent nine days in a sesshin, a Zen Buddhist retreat. At the time I thought it was without doubt a miserable, horrible, cruel, sadistic experience. . . . I got sick. I was paranoid. They sucked me in, seduced my ego by making me feel like I could do it. Then, I got there and they didn't even give me a reward of saying, "Ram Dass, welcome." A guy met me with a clipboard and said, "Dass, Ram; you'll be in the upper bunk in Cabin Three. Here is your robe. Report to the zendo in five minutes." There was a fellow with a stick, and unless you sat in perfect form—which was really uncomfortable—you got beaten. And I was paying money for this! If you tilted, this really fierce character would come up and he'd bow to you, then you'd bow to him, and then you'd lean over to the side and he'd beat you on one shoulder, and then you'd lean over the other way and he'd beat you on the other shoulder, and you'd thank him and he'd thank you.

Five times a day, you'd go in to see the Roshi, a tough Japanese fellow, bald headed. He had a bell and a stick, and he'd ask you ridiculous questions like, "How do you know your Buddha-nature from the sound of clapping hands?" And you'd answer something or other that you'd been thinking about the whole time you were sitting there, knowing you had four more times to go yet today. And he'd say, "Oh, Doctor, you're not doing it right at all. Maybe we should give you your money back, you leave. I had great hopes for you. You're very important, people know you, and you're very famous, but you don't seem to understand this. I think you'd better forget it."

Then he rings his bell, and you leave and you're crushed. Not only are you crushed, but you also have to run back to the place and sit up straight so as not to get beaten. This goes on from two in the morning until ten at night. There's no edge. I spent four days plotting how to be called away on an emergency, some face-saving device. I even tried to hide in the bathroom, but they checked the bathroom. There was simply no place to hide.

Finally, by the fifth day, I didn't give a damn about the Roshi or the whole scene. I went in kind of slouching, thinking, *The hell with it. Let them throw me out,* and he said, "Doctor, how do you know your Buddha-nature through clapping hands?" And I said, "Good morning, Roshi." He said, "AH!!" He was delighted and smiled and then, lest it go to my head, he said, "Now you are becoming a beginning student of Zen!"

Well, it was interesting because just before that, just as I was walking up the path and saying, "Screw it," fire started to pour out of all the bushes and the whole sky became radiant, and I went into this other state. It was like I had been released from this incredible sickness and tension, and I went in and I was having a satori experience. And he kept asking me koan after koan, and the answers kept coming right out. I was right in the moment, and there were no models in my mind. And we just went higher and higher together, and we were both just spinning out.

From then on, the rest of the nine days was ecstasy. The sittings were beautiful, and I was just floating. Suddenly, the perfection of the emptiness of the forms and the impersonality, became my freedom. If I had come to the sesshin and they had said, "Oh, Ram Dass, we're so happy to see you," and I had known who everybody was, it would have occupied my mind in a whole other way. I was freed by the total impersonality of the whole scene.

It's just like any meditation when it's not all bliss and light and we're uncomfortable and it's hot and we're bored and our butts hurt and all that. It's all the same as that sesshin. But we do it because there's something we want bad enough to go through it, to struggle against the forces in us that just want "more."

That's what the *Bhagavad Gita* is about, the battle inside between those two forces. Right until the very end, it's hell. It doesn't get any better; it gets worse because the fire gets hotter and hotter.

You see, once we decide that we really want to go for broke, for perfected truth, once we're being pulled that way in our gut and we finally say, "I don't want anything else. I just want to go" (which is usually a lie, but we're still saying it), that pull, that reaching, draws down upon us all kinds of forces that help that thing happen. That's called grace. There are many beings, both on this plane and on other planes, that are available to guide us and help us, but they don't come unless we want them. Our reaching elicits their help.

The teaching gets fiercer; the fire gets hotter; we start to do it to ourselves because the pull of God is deeper and deeper. At that point just before twelve on our evolutionary clock, the entire universe is within us, and we experience all of the suffering that is connected with form on any plane of existence. We are one with it. By that time, we have worked out all our personal karma or clinging. Now we're aware of the collective nature of the karma. Right at that moment, the pull to twelve o'clock is incredible. To go into twelve o'clock means that we merge back in, that we as consciously separate entities cease. Everything that went on from one minute past twelve until 11:59 was designed for this moment of choice. If we want to be God at this moment, we can merge back in.

But it doesn't matter what choice we make. That may be scary because we wanted it to matter. Most of us are so caught in righteousness, we're afraid of truth. Righteousness would say it matters at 11:59, but truth says it doesn't matter. At 11:59 we have the choice of going back into God, in which case, if we had bodies, they would just sort of disintegrate because there would be nobody in them, or we can stay back in form on this or another plane. Why would we do it?

This is free will in the true sense of free will, not the illusion of free will that we have, for there is no individual karma in this. The only reason a totally free being would choose to stay within the illusion is to relieve the suffering of all beings. This is the time when what's known as "the Bodhisattva Vow" is taken. This is the only moment it's real. Up until then it's phony—it's our karma working out. The moment we choose to come back, we have to push against that force that is drawing us in to merge. We are pushing against God. That is the sacrifice. The sacrifice that Christ made is not the crucifixion. The chance for a conscious being to leave his body is bliss. The sacrifice was leaving the Father in the first place and becoming the Son.

Free beings, realized perfected beings, have that free choice. They are here only because of us, and I mean us, because otherwise we wouldn't meet them. Anybody they meet is by design part of what they're doing to relieve suffering. They are here only as instruments to bring through that nonclinging, nonattached truth, to create a mirror against which we can see where we're holding our secret stash of stuff that is keeping us from being perfected also. These are the beings that bestow the grace. They are the Gods and Goddesses and Gurus on all planes. We all have one of these helpers specifically designed for our karma, but most of us never meet them in this lifetime because we never reach out.

Every night Buddha would look over all the realms, the Buddha-fields, to see who was ready, who looked up, who was reaching, who is saying, "I want to get out," who says, "Know me. Let me out. I'm ready; let's go." Not wanting to want, not phony wanting, but wanting. If we don't reach out, nothing happens. For whom is the despair deep enough?

This game is designed so that within the illusion, where we think there is free will, we've got to reach for it. And we only reach for it when our karma allows us to reach for it. See the predicament? The only real free will there was in the whole clock was at twelve o'clock to one minute past twelve—the free will to go against the system—and at 11:59 to go back into the system. Otherwise all of it was determined by law.

Keep in mind the entire clock is in the realm of metaphor, or relative reality. At twelve o'clock we never were, nothing has happened, nobody is. To answer the question of why did it all begin, one of the answers is it never did. It's just a play of mind, just a play of mind. People who have come this far in this transmission are everywhere between one minute past six and 11:59 and because of the nature of our attachments, we can see only what we can see. We might be sitting next to an 11:59er, and we wouldn't know it, because he doesn't have a sign on him, and the ones that do have signs on them usually aren't real, because they wrote them themselves.

It might turn out that your Aunt Thelma was Buddha. She was cooking chicken soup, and you went to India and Tibet for forty years looking for somebody who looked like Buddha. You totally despaired, and in the despair, you gave up all your hope and all your models. You come home, and you walk in and there she is. You look, and you fall on your face before this brilliant light, and she says, "Have some soup." The pure Buddha, the mind that is clear of attachment, exists anywhere in perfect harmony with all the forces around it.

And to complete this clock image, I might add that for some of us, it has become time to awaken, and for others, it's later than we think.

Chapter 5

Levels of Reality

It's useful to understand the various levels of reality, to examine the perceptual fields that different beings have, to see what different realities look like. Imagine that we have a little dial right next to our eyes and that we can change the channels of our realities. These channels are not to be confused with the chakras. Set the dial on the first channel, and we look around the room and we see men and women. We see that some are tall and some are short and some are light and some are dark, some are beautiful and some are not beautiful, some are blond and some are brunette, some are fat and some are thin, some turn us on and some don't. That's the physical reality.

Somebody says, "Who was in the room?" We say, "Well, there were about an even number of men and women. And they were mainly young between the ages of . . ." If we were social scientists, we might say, "There were so many endomorphs, so many ectomorphs, and so many mesomorphs." If we're in social action, we might say, "There was a minority of blacks, there were so many Hispanics, and there were so many . . ." If we were primarily sexually oriented within that domain, we would see everybody in one of three categories: either potentially makeable, a competitor with us for someone who is potentially makeable, or irrelevant. And that's a very dominant theme in the *Playboy, Penthouse, Oui* clientele, which involves a large percentage of this society. That's what's real for them; the rest is all trips. When the dial is set on the first channel, when we look at the world, we see the physical material environment.

If we're in the clothing business, we walk down the street and see what everybody's wearing. That's the reality for us. And if someone asked, "Who was it that just passed?" we'd say, "I passed a gown from Bergdorfs," or "Shoes from Saks and a hat from Filene's that was on sale last week." Or if we're preoccupied with our bodies when we walk down the street, you know what we see? Everybody else's bodies. People who are busy being short are preoccupied with how tall everyone is. People who don't like their noses notice everybody else's noses.

Flip to the second channel, and we're in the psychological domain. If we were very technical people, we would now look at everybody in terms of the Minnesota Multiphasic Personality Inventory or the Rorschach inkblot test. We are now looking at happy, sad, achievers, anxious neurotics, manic-depressives, enthusiasts, spiritual seekers. Eager, depressed, hearty, happy, sad, lucky—a whole lot of psychological attributes. For many of us, that is the reality in which we live. And who we are is our personality. We spend time analyzing and therapizing them, patting them, damning them, feeding their guilt, their shame, their unworthiness. It happens that the psychologies come in bodies, but we don't even notice the bodies—we're too busy with the psychologies and personalities. When we meet people we say, "Our personalities do well together." It's the only reality. We don't notice bodies. We don't look up; we don't look down. We're all psychology. That's the personality level.

Then there's another channel. Flick. Now the world is twelve categories and their various permutations. There's a Leo; there's an Aries. "I know you're a Sagittarius. I can tell by the way you walk." We've now done an astral fix, a new game of individual differences. We now know people's subtle bodies, which are inside their physical bodies, and we know about something that lies behind their personalities—a planetary reality, the archetypal and mythic reality. It's another game of individual differences. But the third channel allows us to re-perceive the first and second channels. We're now using one set of individual differences to free us from another.

What do you say, once more? Flick, fourth channel. Now when we look into another person's eyes, what we see is another person looking back at us. "Are you in there? I'm in here. Far out. How did you get into that one?" Now we see another being who is just like us, another entity trapped inside the illusion of all these packages of individual differences—body, personality, astrology. And the eyes, the windows of the soul, meet, and we say, "What's it like being in there?"

You'll notice that when we meet other people, we're meeting them at all these different levels. If, for instance, you're a girl, and you're on the personality level of reality, but you happen to have a very beautiful body from a cultural point of view, and everybody you meet sees only your body, you might say, "Why doesn't any-body want me for my personality?" That's because you're such a strong stimulus on the first channel that nobody can get to channel two. Or you're sitting on the fourth channel, which is just a soul inside all this stuff—but most people are busy responding to you as a personality, a body, an astrology, though every now and then you'll walk down the street and look into somebody's eyes, and there's somebody else who's looking back at you. They're not coming on, they're not trying to seduce you, change you, buy you, collect you, proselytize you, reject you, judge you, or anything. They're just there. "You're here, I'm here. Far out place to meet, isn't it?" It's just beings meeting inside these packages of individual differences. And no longer are these individual differences the reality that is so solid. They're just like shirts and jackets and sweaters. "That's a pretty personality you're wearing. Where did you get that one?" "I bought it in Gestalt therapy. It's primal scream." But it's still separate. We're still separate from each other.

Once more. One more channel. Now what do we see when we look at another person? It's as if we have two mirrors facing each other with nothing in between. It's itself, looking at itself looking at itself. In that reality there is only one of us here in drag. One is appearing to be the many in order to play out this game. We are all the Ancient One. We are the One. And the One becomes the many—for the play, for the sport, for the dance—and we can get lost in the many in realities one, two, three, or four. But on channel five, there is only one of us, not intellectual or metaphorical. In that reality, we *are* one. Every reality up to this point is an equally valid, relative, symbolic reality. They're all real, but they're all just relatively real. One of them is no more real than any other one. The way in which we're the One is no more real than the way in which we're the many.

Flick to the next channel and what happens is that everything out there disappears, and we disappear, and there's nobody looking at anything. The whole television disappears. It all goes back into the Void from whence it came. It returns to the formless—to that which lies behind the One. It is what God is—not the concept of God, but God Itself. In Buddhism, it is Nirvana; in Hinduism, it is Brahma; in Taoism, it is the eternal Tao. It is the Aum, the unmanifest universe. It is why the Hebrews write *God* as *G-d,* because it isn't speakable; it is the unspeakable source of it all.

On this sixth channel, the whole subject-object universe dissolves. And it all just is, but without form. Because in order to know form, we have to be separate from it. To enter into the formless that lies beyond the form, out of which the form comes, and back into which it returns, is to touch upon the reality out of which all relative realities arise. As we enter into the realm of channel six, the last moment of recognition of any kind of self-consciousness is the realization that all of channels one through five were creations of mind. A liberated being is a being who is free to be in, but not attached to, any of the realities. It is a being who can enter into the ocean of channel six and yet return into form. This is a being who has all of the channels available at once, though he or she may attend to them somewhat sequentially.

Each one of those channels is a reality. But when we're totally in one of those, it is our absolute reality. You're somebody sitting here reading this book; that's a reality. But is that any more or less real than the reality that there is only one of us reading? It's just a different level of reality, a different flick of the dial.

Part of the process of awakening that we're going through is the recognition that the realities that we thought were absolute are only relative. Since, as we flip the dial, we go toward more and more energy, and more and more fineness of vibration, when we meet a new reality, we experience an intensity that makes us think that the new reality is more real than the old reality. We are living simultaneously on a number of levels, living out the karma of our separateness on plane after plane after plane. But we, as self-conscious entities, are identified at any one moment most likely with only one of those planes. Thus, to define ourselves as being within any one plane of this baklava is to impose a limiting condition, and we are then less than free. Even to consider channels one through five as real is just an imposition of the intellect—describing structures. The intellect goes up only a few levels, and then it becomes a limiting system. When we go back about three or four planes, there are no time or space dimensions. Past, present, future, here and there, are all here. The Buddha looked back over his last ninety-nine thousand incarnations, just like that, and saw them all clearly and simultaneously, because he did not have to be limited by his linear mind. Part of the key to acknowledging our other identities, then, is the process of allowing other kinds of knowing to be real for us, other than the ways we know through our five senses and our thinking minds. Sometimes we call it using the intuitive mind. Heinlein, in *Stranger in a Strange Land,* called it grokking.

Now, the fact that we were born into this plane, which exists in this place at this moment, means that we were born into channels one and two, though we also exist on channels three, four, five, and six. Most of the people around us who we have grown up with take channels one and two as absolute reality. Thus when we go into channels three, four, five, and six, they say, "Get real. Get your feet back on the ground. Come back to reality."

People who acknowledge channels three, four, five, and six are often treated as psychotic. "You have flipped out of conventional reality." For someone who sees through the game of relative realities, the clinging to any reality at all as "the reality" is really the definition of insanity. I once visited my brother in a mental hospital. I sat in a room with him and his psychiatrist. He thought he was Christ, and the psychiatrist thought he was a psychiatrist, and each of them was convinced that the other one was insane.

Most of the experiences that we have sought in our lives have been attempts to enter the universal oneness of channel five—total orgasm—the moment in which there is no longer somebody having sex with somebody, when it's merely the universe happening. That moment of perfect flow, in which all separateness has disappeared, is the moment when we are home again, when we know where we belong, when we have returned into the One, when all of the tension that is created by the separateness has, for a moment, dissipated. Most of us know that at the moment of orgasm, all of our neuroses are irrelevant—not the moment before or the moment after, but for that exact moment. For somebody who is capable of living in channel five, that moment of orgasm, of total merging with the One, is a reality all the time.

In order to be open to this merging, many of us who have smoked pot or taken acid, or had other vehicles for overriding our programs, know that we can set aside our programs for a moment and enter into the higher channels; but after a while, we come down, and, as a result, we get very frustrated. What brings us down is our attachment to the models or programs about who we think we are and how we think the world is—these habits of mind.

Many of us are getting to the point in our spiritual journey where we are no longer trying to get high, for we know how to do that. We are trying to *be*. And being includes everything. We now recognize that if there is anything at all that can bring us down—anything—our house is built upon sand, and there is fear. And where there is fear, we aren't free. Thus we become motivated to confront the places in ourselves that bring us down—not only to confront them, but to create situations in which to bring them forth. That's quite a turnaround from a mentality that says, "I just want to get high." This new mentality says, "I want to get done; I want to be liberated in this very birth. I've seen how it could be; I'm tired of just seeing previews of coming attractions; I want the main feature."

This mentality is quite different. Now, when there is depression, instead of running and hiding from the depression and trying to grab the next high, we turn around and we look at the depression as though we were looking the devil in the eye, and we say to the depression, "Come on, depression. Do your trip, because you're just a depression, and here I am." We can do this because we are just a little bit connected to channel four, which lies beyond channel two, and the psychological channel is where depressions are.

To a being living on the fourth channel, what do you suppose sexual anxieties are all about? "Was I good? Was it enough? Did I satisfy her or him? Will it happen too soon? Can I get it up? Should I fake it? Am I frigid? Will it be real?" Those worries are on the first and second channels. They're not "not-real," but how different it would feel if our identities were rooted in channel four, if we were able to say, "I am a soul that has taken incarnation in a body that has this particular sexual habit." We even arrive at the space where we are able to look back at our entire lives of neuroses and suffering and say, "Look at how perfect that has been in bringing me to this moment."

So we have the paradox that, on channels one and two and three, there is an incredible melodrama going on, and we are actors within it. There is a great deal of suffering, and when we're locked into channel one, and we're hungry, and there's no food— that's real suffering. It's not fake suffering. But from channels four and five, we can look at one, two, and three, and look at all the individual differences and at all of the melodrama and say, "Look at the perfection of the dance. Look at the perfection of the flow of the Divine Law—including the will of man that can go against the Will of God. Look at the perfection of it all."

But it's not freedom for the being *attached* to channels four or five who, when you're hurting, says, "It's not real, don't worry. You're the Buddha. It's all an illusion." That's no more liberated than the person who's caught in one, two, and three and says, "There's only pain and suffering everywhere, and it's hell. Life is terrible and ugly." The free being lives within all those realities simultaneously. He understands paradoxically that when there is suffering, we do everything we can to alleviate it, while at the same time, the suffering is perfection itself, and our doing everything we can to alleviate it is also part of the perfection. Ultimately we understand when we are free to move without attachment from level to level of reality, that the only reason we stay in form is to alleviate suffering or to bring others to the light, to consciousness, to liberation, to God. What a paradox! Is it perfect? Sure. Is it hell? Sure. It's both at the same moment. And all of this, too, is at only one level of exploration.

Chapter 6

The Mellow Drama

Perhaps there will come a time in the not-too-distant future when we will be able to gather and sit in silence, not in expectation, but in fulfillment. We will recognize who we are, that we are beings of the spirit, and we will seek that food which feeds our soul. Our intellects will be available, but at rest, and our hearts will be filled with the love of Christ, that flowing, conscious love. We will be done with romanticizing our own journey, examining ourselves self-consciously to see how we're doing. We won't have to compare or assess whether we're getting enough, for we will trust our hearts.

For many of us, that time is now. For others, the faith is still too flickery. In lectures I've spoken about phony holy—that is, appearing holier than we are. Here I would speak more about phony unholy. Many of us are higher than we are admitting to. We create molds or models of our reality that keep us from recognizing ourselves. For many of us, our spiritual model was "the good life." *Good* meant a life consciously lived—simple, righteous, not ripping off people or the environment, socially conscious, keeping our scene straight, and being a person of peace—not lost in our frustrations, in violence, in anger, in lust. That's pretty good. To have found that level in this society puts us already in the tiny part of 1 percent. But even when we get all of that together, there's something in us that's yearning, because no matter how subtly beautiful our models are, they still define us within worldly concepts. But in truth, though we live in this world, we are not solely of this world. We have learned to live in this world, but we have not yet fully recognized where we come from or who we are, for to explore beyond the world is a bit like stepping off into the Void; it's like diving off a diving board when we're afraid of diving.

But if we're asking for freedom, if terms like *liberation,* or *realization,* or *enlightenment,* or *living in God* have any meaning to us, then leading the good life is just part way home. Many of us, in this very lifetime, have come from tremendous preoccupation with our neuroses, with our achievements, with our careers, with our melodramas, and we've arrived at a place where we can laugh. We can say, "Isn't it a mellow drama!"—not just someone else's, but our own. Some of us are not as busy being neurotic as the general population, because we've begun to take our personalities a little less seriously. They're there, just like our bodies are—we comb them, wash them, clean them up, dress them, move them here and there, love them, caress them, stimulate them, get rushes off of them. They're our traveling temples. Our personalities, too, are just another shawl, cloaks. But there are a good number of us who realize that we are not just either body or personality.

We have been together for so many years now, going through so many trips together. And I've hung in, as many of you have.

But personal history has become a kind of limiting condition. Now I'd rather just talk about how it is when you are free to play with God for the rest of your life.

But still some things need to be said. I'd like to just play out the "his-story" a little bit. In 1970, I had been back from India about three years, *Be Here Now* was just about to come out, and I was pretty freaked by how much I was lost in the world. I went running back to my Guru in India.

When I arrived there, he asked me, "What are you doing here?"

And I said, "Well, I'm not pure enough to do whatever it is I am supposed to be doing—I don't even know what it is, but I'm not pure enough to do it."

He hit me on the head, pulled my beard, and said, "You will be."

For a year and a month, I followed him around India, and every time I'd go to see him, he'd throw me out. He'd let others stay with him for months, but I'd come, and he'd say, "*Jao!* (Go away!) Go to Delhi." Go here, go there. I had many adventures, and each time I'd come back, and I'd say, "Maharaj-ji, you promised you'd make me pure enough." And he'd just laugh or say, "You will be."

Finally, I was being thrown out of India by the Indian government because of visa problems. Let me explain that when I got to India that time, Maharaj-ji said, "How long do you want to stay?"

I said, "I don't know. I want to stay forever." Which wasn't true—you can only take so much dysentery—but I thought I should say it.

And he said, "How about March?" This was February.

I said, "You mean a month?"

Maharaj-ji said, "All right, a year from March."

So it just turned out that it was exactly a year from March when the Indian government threw me out. Now, you can see no obvious cause and effect between Maharaj-ji's prediction and the action of the Indian government, but once you've begun to see how the game works, you wouldn't trust anybody as far as you could throw them. You don't know who works for whom anymore. It isn't even done on this plane; that's what's so bizarre about it.

As the Indian government was about to throw me out, I said, "Maharaj-ji, you promised." I assumed that when I was pure enough, I would feel pure. I didn't know what it was going to feel like, but I knew it would feel different than the way I was feeling. So he said, "Here, eat this mango." Well, I've read a lot of holy books, so I figured, *This is* the *mango*. I took it into the bathroom so I wouldn't have to share it with anybody. I didn't know whether to plant the seed so that I could have more, or whether this would be enough. I ate the mango, and nothing happened. It was just a good mango.

Then I was leaving for America, and he said, "I would never let Ram Dass do anything wrong in America." I figured, *Okay, I'll hold him to it.* So I came back to America and started to do my thing some more. And slowly the pulls of the world started to get at me. It had been easy to be very focused on God sitting in a temple in India. Particularly that year. There had been a fire ceremony. At the end of the nine-day ceremony, you take whatever you want to get rid of, put it in a coconut, and throw it into the fire. I wanted to get rid of my lust. After all, I was forty years old at that point: enough, already! It had been my total preoccupation for thirty years. If I hadn't had enough by then, there obviously wasn't enough, so I decided to give it up. So I gave it to the fire.

The next day was the Ram Lila. They were going to burn a huge straw effigy of Ravana. Ravana's the bad guy in the *Ramayana;* he was a huge ego and had ten heads, all filled with desire. You could throw into the effigy whatever within you was Ravana-like. I figured, "Well, I'll be doubly safe and throw my lust into Ravana." They took the torch, and they lit Ravana—he was sitting on a huge chair—and they lit him right between the legs. Very symbolic. It turned out it was Yom Kippur that night, so to be triply certain, I covered that base too.

For three months, it seemed to have worked. But then I was sitting on a double-decker bus in London, and I noticed my eyes looking down at the sidewalk, following an attractive being down the street. And I thought, *Uh-oh, here we go again.* So it was that I returned to the West, ready again to be a spiritual teacher.

I was planning to return to India again in two years. That would have been in 1974, but Maharaj-ji died before that. Now, when Maharaj-ji dropped his body, my intellect said to me, "Where could he go?" because sometimes in the past I would sit with him, and I would see that physical body, and then I would quiet down in meditation, and I would feel his presence on another plane. And then I would shatter that one and meet him on yet another plane. My body would start to shake with shakti, from the amount of energy coming from these different planes. I would move through plane after plane of meeting him in different ways.

I remembered the story you've perhaps heard about Ramana Maharshi, who was dying, and his devotees said, "Babaji, please don't leave us. Heal yourself."

And he said, "No, this body is used up."

And they said, "Don't leave us, don't leave us."

And Ramana Maharshi said, "Don't be silly; where could I go?" Which seemed to me to be the most concise statement of the whole illusion of body. But somewhere inside me was a whole different story. I knew that I wasn't cooked; Maharaj-ji was the cook, and he had just left.

When they burned Maharaj-ji's body, different people saw different things at the burning. Most people were crying and wailing and feeling, like I was, that we had lost our Guru. There was one man who stood by the fire, just laughing and singing, singing, "Sri Ram Jai Ram Jai Jai Ram," all through the night.

The next day they asked him, "Why were you laughing and singing?"

And he said, "Maharaj-ji was sitting up laughing, and Ram was pouring ghee, clarified butter, on his head so he'd burn faster; and Brahma, Vishnu, and Siva, and all the gods and goddesses were raining down flowers, and everybody was happy."

Now, was that man deluded, or was that reality? One woman saw Maharaj-ji get up on his elbow and wave at her as if to say, "Don't get upset, Ma," and then lie back down and get burned.

For two years, then, I had been incorporating what I'd learned from my Guru, living and teaching as best I could, hoping that his "I would never let Ram Dass do anything wrong in America" meant that my impurities would not create karma for other beings. I was doing certain things to keep myself as straight as I knew how. I had a Volkswagen camper, and I would go off, say, to the desert in Arizona for six weeks of seclusion. I was cleaning up a lot of my game that way. During those years I was taking acid once each year to find out what I was forgetting, to uncover any subtle ways in which I was conning myself. One year I took it in the Mid-America Motel in Salina, Kansas; that was my mid-America trip. Although I continually felt Maharaj-ji's presence, I still wanted to experience it even more strongly, because he is my way, and I wanted to get on with it.

In the summer of 1974, I was at Naropa Institute teaching a course on the *Bhagavad Gita*, a course for which I felt Maharaj-ji was giving his blessings. At Naropa, I was part of a whole other scene, because Trungpa Rinpoche represented a different lineage. I found myself floundering a little bit because my own path was so amorphous compared to the tightness of the Tibetan tradition. Trungpa and I did a few television shows together. We did one about lineages, and I felt bankrupt. I had Maharaj-ji's transmission of love and service, but I knew nothing about his history. I didn't know how to talk about what came through me in terms of a formal lineage. I was also getting caught in more worldly play, and I felt more and more depressed and hypocritical. So by the end of the summer, I decided to return to India. I didn't know what I'd find, but I'd go anyway. I knew I was different than I had been ten years before, but I was still not cooked, and what we owe each other is to get cooked.

Driving east, I stopped overnight in Pennsylvania at a motel where I was planning to watch the House Judiciary Committee hearings on television, but a storm put out the electricity. It was too early to go to sleep, so there was nothing left to do but meditate. After about fifteen or twenty minutes, Maharaj-ji came to me in a vision. He looked just as he had always looked. He laughed and spoke to me. It's interesting—he spoke only Hindi, and my Hindi was very bad. In India there was always somebody translating. But on these other levels, the transmission is in thought forms, and then it comes out in whatever language you think in. So he said to me, in very good English, "You don't have to go to India. Your teachings will be right here." It was so vivid, and so real that at that precise moment, I decided not to go to India. I decided to go to New Hampshire, meditate a month or so in a cabin, clean out my head, and see what would happen next.

On the following day, passing through New York City, I called Hilda Charlton to say hello. She told me there was a woman in Brooklyn I should meet. When I resisted because I wanted to be alone, she told me that this woman said that my Guru was sitting in her basement.

Of course I decided to stay one more night, and the next day I went with Hilda to see this lady named Joya. We went down into the basement of her home, and there she was, sitting in what Hilda said was samadhi. And I checked: I could find no breath or pulse. She was like a rock. She was a very unusual looking woman. She had long false eyelashes, heavy mascara, and a low-cut dress. Maharaj-ji was an old man in a blanket, but after all, I'd given up having models about what packages the next message is supposed to come in.

Finally she came down, looked at me, and said, "What the fuck do you want?"

Hilda said, "Oh, dear, this is Ram Dass," which didn't seem to make any impression on this lady at all. She said, "I don't care who the hell he is. Does that old man over there belong to you?"

I looked, and there was a blanket with nothing on it. So I said, "I don't know."

She said, "He's buggin' me. Get him the hell out of here."

Then her consciousness shifted just a bit, and she went into a very light trance, and suddenly Maharaj-ji seemed to be speaking to me through her. He was talking about things that he and I had been discussing in India when I had seen him last, little matters about maintenance of the temples in India and all kinds of very picayune stuff that she probably could not know and I hadn't even remembered. She came back from that plane, but, as she explained, she was not conversant across planes, so she didn't know what had just happened. And I was pleased, because this experience—following so closely the vision in the Pennsylvania motel—seemed the answer to my prayers.

A few months later, I moved to New York City, where, for fifteen months, I studied intensively with Joya. The teachings had a bizarre intensity that it is difficult to convey. From five a.m. until one or two a.m. each day, it was like being caught in a tornado or tossed in a giant clothes dryer. One had to either get out or give up. Surrender was ordained an absolute necessity to experience the higher teachings of this quite unusual teacher. Surrender and devotion were methods I had opened my heart to through the teachings of my Guru, so this process was just a deeper letting go—a letting go of even my resistance to much of what seemed to go against common sense.

At this time I also received ghastly reports from various of Joya's closest followers that my resistance was causing Joya bleeding and intense psychic pain. There was no alternative but to suspend all judgment and surrender into these teachings, to simply allow the teaching to come through and burn away all my preconceptions of what a teacher should be or how a teaching should be conveyed. And I let go into what I deeply believed to be a pure transmission. And as I surrendered ever more deeply to those teachings, I stated publicly that, as Joya had professed, she was an enlightened being—a statement that I came to regret. The intensity of the confrontation (often twenty hours a day) forced my subtle ego defenses to the surface. And Joya, in a Kali-esque way, pounced on these impurities and magnified them until I had to let go or get out. I let go of these impurities as fast as I could, and I hung in as best I was able. This was just the fire of purification that my chronic case of unworthiness was seeking.

The intensity of the dramatics and the brilliance of the staging and props created a reality that made me ready to believe the bizarre assertion that a Jewish housewife and mother of three who was married to an Italian Catholic businessman in Brooklyn was in fact Ms. Big, the creative force of the universe. Joya represented herself as an actual form of Kali and a number of other cosmic identities as well, including Athena; Sri Mata Brahma, the Mother of the Universe; and Tara, the Tibetan Goddess of Tantra. It was a hard act to follow.

Several hundred of us were seduced into this reality by a combination of her powerful charisma, her chutzpah, and the fact that she seemed often to go into deep trance states with a cessation of bodily functions; also, she reported that she had manifested the stigmata, and she certainly knew things that a tenth-grade-educated person would not be expected to know. The stage was well set, and we went for it because our greed and our spiritual materialism led us very much to want to believe it.

In the beginning, Joya spent much time in trance states, in which she apparently functioned as a medium. Through her came many seductively rich teachings from biblical figures, Hasidic, Hindu, and Buddhist wise men and women of the past, or from beings on other planes. Her voice and language often shifted from unschooled Brooklynese to exquisite poetry that poured forth for hours at a time. I was breathless with the richness of these moments.

I was led more and more to surrender to the reality of the entire scene, because we were told that it was only through such total loving surrender by those around her that these higher teachings could come forth. She told me that some of my teachers at that time were such august spiritual figures as Jethro (Moses's father-in-law), Padmasambhava, and Lao Tzu, as well as Ramakrishna, Christ, Mary, Nityananda, an early Kabbalah teacher, Kali, and Durga. Having never been around people in trance states, this whole scene really astounded me. I was fully seduced by the whole melodrama, like a tourist, open-mouthed, watching a fakir do the Indian rope trick.

Joya kept reiterating that she had come to earth only to be an instrument for my preparation as a world spiritual leader and that ultimately she would sit at my feet. It sounded a little grandiose because, oddly enough, each day I felt myself more and more becoming just nobody special. There were moments when I felt a bit like Krishnamurti being herded toward leadership of the Order of the Star just before he resigned, leaving fifty thousand members who thought he was the new world leader with a message that they should look within and not seek the Dharma anywhere outside of themselves.

A deep concern in the period just before I met Joya was that I was not yet free of my attachments to sexuality. After a long and intense bisexual history, I still found that my perceptions were being colored by my sexual desires. I could afford to be patient about my own purification from sexual clinging, but in view of my public role, I was uneasy that any sexual preoccupations on my part would subtly contaminate those I worked with, either in lectures or individually, and thus reinforce their own attachments and suffering. Despite the fact that Maharaj-ji said, "I would never let Ram Dass do anything wrong in America," the persistence of these sexual preoccupations led me to question Maharaj-ji's meaning and deeply yearn to clean up my sexual act. In view of how many years I had been trying to get free of these sexual clingings, including offering my lust into the sacrificial fires of India, I had given up hope of ever knowing freedom in this lifetime. The sexual karma just seemed too heavy.

I had read of the Tantric initiations in certain Tibetan sects for just this purpose. The monk would go through a series of ritual openings working with a dakini, a heaven-realm woman. Mostly these were young women who had been prepared from childhood to serve in these rituals without any personal involvement or clinging to the sensual aspect of the ritual. In my fantasies I was hoping that at some point, I too would be introduced to such teachings and through such conscious rituals with a disciplined guide become unattached once and for all to these desires.

And now I was presented with a woman teacher, who within a few months after the commencement of the training, began to focus on my sexuality. As I opened more and more, assured by her of her perfect nonattachment to any desire system, I felt a new hope that my dream of purification was finally manifesting through this teaching. I plunged headlong into the tornado, casting caution and doubt to the winds.

Perhaps the most important of all the considerations affecting my deep involvement with this teaching was that Maharaj-ji had again and again said to me, "See the world as the Mother, and you will know God." He often was heard to be repeating the word *Ma* over and over again. He had a shrine built to Durga, an aspect of the Mother. All of this Mother devotion made me feel a bit like an outsider. My own feelings about mothers were colored by the relationship with my own mother and my training as a Freudian therapist and theorist. To be in love with a universal mother just wasn't happening yet for me. I yearned to understand this aspect of devotion, for I knew that devotion to the Mother, just as devotion to Hanuman, the servant of God for whom I had overwhelming love, was a part of the lineage of my Guru. Sooner or later I felt I would find a way into a devotional relationship with the Mother. When I came to New York City and started to study with Joya and enter her matriarchal reality, I felt that at last I had come into the teaching I had sought for so long—particularly when Joya further professed to be the Divine Mother herself.

The fact that Joya continually spoke about Maharaj-ji and implied his presence by seeming to carry on conversations with an astral Maharaj-ji whom I could not see, fed into my longing and my somewhat shaky faith that, though Maharaj-ji had left his body, he was still around to guide my spiritual journey.

Joya seemed to have great difficulty staying in her body and would, at the slightest provocation, go stiff as a board. Efforts to keep her in her body, to keep her from just leaving her body behind and going on to other realms, consumed much of our time together. There was a jewel that Joya wore around her neck that Hilda had invested with a mantra to bring her down. When Hilda touched the stone, Joya usually came down, but with the pain, so she said, of a thousand razor blades cutting through her. This was in turn very painful to all of us. We therefore went to great lengths to surrender to Joya's every whim so as not to be responsible for this painful drama.

With her increasing feeling of power, she also cast aside Hilda. Hilda, while not being a very strong source of teaching, had, as Joya's compatriot, generated with her astral carryings-on the necessary climate of semi-hysteria to sustain Joya's melodrama.

But it was becoming increasingly apparent that what seemed to have begun as a spontaneous mediumistic opening was just too much energy and power for an unprepared individual with power needs and love needs of her own. It seems that the temptation to misuse the trust and power for personal aggrandizement and emotional reinforcement was just too much for her to overcome. Instead of remaining an empty vessel, which on occasion contained the wisdom of the ages, Joya claimed the contents as her own; indeed, she claimed no longer to be just the vessel but the source of the messages that came through—it was a bit like a cup which, filled with seawater, claims to be the ocean itself.

There were just too many "signals," like the moment Joya and I were hanging out, and the telephone rang. She picked up the receiver and in a pained whisper said, "I can't talk now. I'm too stiff," and let the receiver drop. Then, without hesitation, she continued our conversation as if nothing had happened. I realized how many times I had been at the other end of the phone.

And I became bored.

For several months I interpreted my boredom and heretical thoughts as my ego desperately defending against the ultimate surrender.

But no matter how I rationalized, my doubts and boredom grew. The tantric exercises no longer seemed productive. I began to experience Joya as another person with attachments. So I began to entertain the possibility that these feelings were cues that I was finished with this teaching and should leave.

Increasingly there came the recognition that though all these planes and beings are simply fascinating, it just isn't the same as liberation. There was more power, more light, more energy; shakti just pouring through us; beings appearing to us, great teachings, wisdom, knowledge. But I noticed that my power trips were still there . . . still active. I watched myself think, *Boy, I waited a long time for this*. And then there's another plane and another. But it's just another space, and attachment to that space is just more suffering. As the Sixth Zen Patriarch reiterates, "Develop a mind which clings to naught." All these planes are listed in the yoga sutras. But they're all just stuff. They are interesting and useful to loosen our hold on this plane and to transmute and to burn out stuff, but ultimately it's just more stuff— because experiences in meditation and shakti experiences, just like experiences on acid, ultimately must be let go of. If we can give it all up, then we just finish with the karma. Then we can go beyond polarity, beyond pleasure and pain, and awaken out of the illusion of our separateness.

And we begin to understand that we have taken birth in order to go through a series of experiences until we transcend the dualism of experiencer and experience. We reside in being, not becoming—until we can *be*, rather than just know, the teachings, so that we *are* the teachings.

By the end of this period, I felt I had finished my work with Joya and many of the beings who taught through her. It just wasn't what I needed anymore. It was like trying to find out how many angels can fit on the head of a pin. Finally, the only thing you can do is become an angel and see how many of your friends can hang out on the pin with you.

My doubts grew faster than I could consume them. Joya had changed a great deal in the year. She came to resent having beings speak through her and refused to serve as a medium. Thus while she still had great shakti and charisma, her lectures became merely the reflections of the culture in which she had grown up, sprinkled with spiritual homilies.

As the reality crumbled, I began to see the painful backstage life of the actors, and I attempted to bow out as gracefully and as lovingly as possible. Maharaj-ji had warned us that no matter what we did, we should never put another person out of our heart. I waited until my love was strong, but when I tried to leave, it was very difficult, and it became apparent that I was involved in a system that had no escape clause. I had to push against the system, though there was very little support for such action. And I began to see the similarity between what I was experiencing and the stories I had heard about other movements, such as the Rev. Moon's group, the so-called Jesus Freaks, and the Krishna Consciousness scene. Each seemed a total reality that turned involvement into a commitment that disallowed change.

My leaving Joya was part of a large exodus of disillusioned followers, including some who had served in her home. As the refugees who left the front lines exchanged stories, a tapestry of falsehood and misuse of the truth started to unravel. It seemed that her incredible energies came not solely from spiritual sources but were also enhanced by energizing pills. Her closest confidants now confessed many times they were ordered to call me to report terrible crises they knew to be untrue. They complied because Joya had convinced them that it was for my own good. Such stories of deception came thick and fast. I had been had.

Some of what I had said in lectures or articles about Joya's teachings were just not true. I came away with egg on my beard. But of more significance than my embarrassment was the issue of truth. In a sense I found myself in a position not unlike that of Mahatma Gandhi when, having initiated a large protest march in which many thousands were involved, called his lieutenants after the first day's march and cancelled the protest. They objected strongly, saying that after all this work and effort, he couldn't do this. He answered, "My commitment is to truth, not consistency."

I was confronted with the dilemma of how to communicate to the many who had put their deepest trust in me, in much the same manner I had put my deep trust in Joya, and how not to let them down in the same manner that I had been so disappointed.

These teachings had their positive side. Many people underwent incredibly deep experiences regarding who they really were during an intense sadhana, which they may not have undertaken without that illusion to draw out the energy and commitment needed to do the work that each must do for himself. Through these teachings, and the leaving of them, many of us gained more strength and compassion, greater openness and a deeper ability to allow the moment to be as it is. For all of this, I am deeply grateful. However, while I and others profited from these teachings, not everybody did. Some seemed to have been hurt and came away from her teaching with despair, cynicism, and paranoia.

The question arises whether there is reason to fear taking teachings because a teacher might not be coming from the purest place. I think we need not fear this, for often students can progress very far; indeed, their purification may be greater than their teacher's, because their intention is purer. I got my karmuppance because of my own spiritual materialism. If our longing for God is pure, that will be our strength. Then, though we may get lost for a time, eventually our inner heart will hear what to do, and all the impurities in our world will just become grist for the mill.

Chapter 7

Lineage

I struggled for a number of years to be a pure eclectic—that is, to be true to each tradition as I was studying it and yet to be strong enough to be able to hold them all within myself, to contain them all. But what I had to do, which most of you have had to do, was to compartmentalize myself into a series of conceptual groupings, so that when you are with the Buddhists, you are Buddha-like; when you are with the Sufis, you are Sufi-like; when you're with the Hindus, you're Hindu-like; when you're with the Christians, you're Christian-like; when you're with the Hasids, you're Hasid-like.

Years ago, we had a retreat at a Benedictine monastery, and there was a gathering of the "big boys." There was Swami Satchidananda, Alan Watts, Sasaki Roshi, Brother David, Pir Vilayat Khan, and on and on and on. We each got a chance to do our specialty, and everybody participated. At four a.m. I was sitting next to Swami Satchidananda, and we were doing zazen. We were working on a koan, "How do you know your Buddha-nature through the sound of a cricket?" Then we were to go in properly with the three bows and the kneeling and the whole ritual to see the Roshi. He sat there with a bell and a stick.

It was the first time I had done this. So all the time we were sitting there "being empty" I was, of course, planning my answer, because I didn't want to make a fool of myself. This was a heavy league to be playing in, you know. So . . . "How do you know your Buddha-nature through the sound of a cricket?" I thought and thought and thought and finally hit on one that I thought would be perfectly appropriate. I came in and Sasaki Roshi said, "Ah, Doctor, how do you know your Buddha-nature through the sound of a cricket?" I cupped my hand to my ear like Milarepa listening to the sounds of the universe. I figured I'm a Jewish Hindu in a Catholic monastery, so I'll give him a Tibetan answer to a Japanese koan. I was really just delighted with my own cuteness. And he looked at me and rang his bell and said, "Sixty percent!" And at that moment, he absolutely had me. He caught me perfectly in my middle-class achievement-oriented identity. We both laughed.

Those moments of connectedness, such as with Sasaki Roshi, on more than one plane simultaneously are very precious—when we meet another human being both in form and out of form, when we are dancing with them and yet we are free of attachment to the roles in the dance.

I had a moment like that with Swami Muktananda when he gave me a mantra, and in an inner room of his temple, the mantra took me up to an astral plane, where I met him again. I looked into his eyes. And when I did, I started to go up and to fly. As I was flying, I started to lose my balance and went to straighten myself out and was immediately brought back to the cave in his temple in which I was meditating. I came staggering out of the cave, just having returned to earth, and met him out in the hallway, and he said to me through his interpreter, "How did you like flying?" He looked at me with a twinkle, which was the twinkle of "You and I just met there. And yet we're here, and we're together at all of these places simultaneously." There was that delight, delight, the delight of that moment. Alan Watts was a person very much into that space of sharing two planes simultaneously, of that kind of delight, as was Carl Jung, it seemed, who would go up and out into these other realms, these other planes of reality. But when he returned, he said something like, "I was always so happy to get back to my family and to earth, to my home from these other states." But that's not total freedom, for to be enlightened means you don't cling anywhere—not to this or to that.

With most of the beings with whom I've had this moment, we could have only a moment. I never knew whether we could only have a moment because there is only the possibility of having a moment or because neither I nor any of us were pure enough to be able to maintain that space continuously. The only person who was always there (though I have never been consistently able to locate him in a time-space "fix") was Maharaj-ji—because no matter where I looked, he was and he wasn't. No matter how high I went, he was always sitting there. No matter where I go, I feel him always present. Now, that could be an opening of my heart specifically to him. Or it could be something else—something about him and his own freedom.

At the beginning of the journey, we are very eclectic. That's what *Be Here Now* is. It's very eclectic . . . a little of this and a little of that—a Buddhist meditation to quiet the mind, some

Sufi dancing to open the body and heart, some Tai Chi when the body's not balanced, some massage to loosen it all up, a mantra as a centering device, many methods to choose from the spiritual smorgasbord.

But there comes a point where the inner pull starts to draw us in the direction of one lineage or another. These could also be called ways or aspects of God; they all go to God, but they all come through slightly different routes. They are our dharmic paths. So for one, the route that would be optimal in this life is to marry and have children and be a householder, coming to God through service in that domain. For another person, that is an adharmic path—it would take them away from God. We cannot conclude that there is any route that is in and of itself the perfect route for each of us. There *is* a route, however, and part of the process of tuning is listening to hear how it all is for us. And what we tune to, ultimately, is the vehicle through which we can sufficiently surrender.

An example of a particular lineage is worship of the Mother. You can see the entire universe of forms, all form, as the Mother. We are all part of the Mother. The Mother has many faces—the Virgin Mary, Durga, Lakshmi, Kali. Some are wrathful; some are tender. Some of us are involved in seeing nature as the Mother— that is Mother Nature. But if we expand it outward, all forms become the Mother, and we end up with the interesting choice of either seeing the world as the Mother or covering the Mother with the world; that is we get caught in her illusion, or Maya, and we don't see the divinity that underlies the stuff of life.

If we cover the Mother with the world, we get lost in the world, and a car is just a car, a television set is a television set, anger is anger, doubt is doubt, and a mother and a father are a mother and a father. If we see behind the world to the Mother, every experience that we have in this lifetime is another aspect or face or quality or tone or movement of the Mother, and, in this reality, we as seekers are relating to the universe as the Mother, constantly learning to love, feed from, interact with, and finally merge with the Mother.

Kali is an aspect of the Divine Mother—but what a mother to have! She's really gruesome. She scares the hell out of most of us. You know why she scares us? Because we want to hold on to who we think we are. She's the fire of purification. She's going to take every single solitary bit of our stash, and what will be left are just pure souls floating up into the One. The minute we're no longer attached to our separateness, to our individual differences, to having the universe the way we think it ought to be, suddenly we don't see the form of Kali. We look right through that one, and we see Durga, the Golden Goddess.

Now, Kali will come after you if you ask her to. If you don't ask her, she won't bother you at all. But if you ask her, she'll confront you with all the "uglies" and then consume your reactions. But if you try to hold on to your reactions, then you're in for it. That's phony holy. If you, in truth, want to give them up, then say, "Here, Kali Ma, you take it."

And how do we make an offering to Kali? The things that don't liberate us, we give up. What do we give up? Unworthiness. We don't need to analyze it; we just give it up. We give up guilt. Guilt isn't going to get us to God. We give up anger. It's not going to free us. Preoccupation with our own melodrama—we give up. Do we want to hold on to it, or do we want to get on with it? God waits patiently. We're the ones in a rush. We want to get on with it, so we give up what we cling to. It's very simple. That's when Maharaj-ji said to me: "Ram Dass, you're angry?" And I answered simply, "Yes." I was very righteously angry. And he said, "Give it up." I hesitated, saying, "But . . ." And he said again, "Just give it up." He looked at me, and I saw who I would be when I had given it up. And it was beautiful.

At first, when we have just started the spiritual journey, every time we are confronted with all the things we're afraid of—disasters or accidents or we get mugged or we get raped or we lose our job or something "awe-ful" happens—we say, "Oh, get away from me. I want happiness. I want pleasure. I didn't know this was part of the bargain." But later on, as we become more conscious of where the journey is going, we say, "If this is what is coming down the pike, I'll work with it." That's the moment when we recognize that suffering can be seen as grace. And at that moment we become invulnerable, because what's anybody to do to us, the Real Us, anyway?

We discover the way in which suffering is the fire of purification: that only when we are lost in our ego do we damn our suffering. When we are souls yearning to be free, we use our suffering, and we use our pleasure. We use it all to get to God, to get liberated. And we begin to notice that our suffering awakens us more than our pleasure. If we seek out pain, we are called masochists. So we don't seek it out because that wouldn't be honest on the psychological level of reality. But when it comes along, we work with it.

"Ah, cancer." As a being in a body, the temple of my soul for this incarnation, I will do my best to heal it, but I will work with the cancer whether I am healed or not, as a vehicle for awakening. A conscious being uses everything. Nothing goes down the disposal—including the moment of death, which can be the most profound moment of the incarnation for growth and awakening when we are ready to use it that way.

When we don't get so lost in our melodramas, we stop creating more karma for ourselves. Letting go is the act of purification. So all the stuff Buddhists call the Five Hindrances, or the Ten Fetters—anger, sloth and torpor, agitation, ill will, greed, lust—all those obvious ones, and all those subtle ones like attachment to fine material-plane things like astral entities—we finally get so greedy to get done that we just want to get rid of the stuff. Instead of spending years analyzing it or therapizing it, like playing with our feces, we just want to get done—we just want to give it all up.

My own lineage is reflected in the name Ram Dass, which means "servant of God." It's a path of devotion to God/Guru, and the expression of that devotion is through service to all beings. Mother Teresa reflected this lineage when she spoke of serving the lepers in the streets of Calcutta as serving "Christ in all his distressing disguises."

The figure in Hinduism most closely associated with this lineage is Hanuman, the monkey God, who is totally one-pointed in his devotional service to Ram (God). Hanuman has great powers through his love of Ram, and in the *Ramayana,* we learn how he uses these powers to help others regain their health, their faith, their rightful place in the harmony of things, and their connection to God. This spiritual path that Hanuman represents is also called Karma Yoga and has much subtlety to it. For example, when Ram asks Hanuman, "Who are you, Hanuman?" Hanuman answers, "When I don't know who I am, I serve you. When I know who I am, I am you."

For me, my Guru, Neem Karoli Baba (Maharaj-ji), is Hanuman and is Ram. Ramana Maharshi said that God, Guru, and the true Self are one and the same. I experience that, through my ever-deepening intimacy and love for Maharaj-ji. Despite the fact that he left his physical body in 1973, I increasingly experience his grace, which seems to be freeing me from fear. I have described him and my relationship to him in over one thousand stories in the book *Miracle of Love*. It continues to amaze and delight me how hundreds of readers who never met him when he was in his body have experienced, after reading that book, dreams and visions of him, and they feel such a strong sense of his presence that their spiritual journey is being guided by him.

Since 1967, when I first asked Maharaj-ji how to become enlightened, he has said at various times, "Love everyone," "Feed everyone," and "Serve everyone." These words have served as a guiding prescription for action in my life. Because all of my service in the world is offered at his feet, the action brings me ever closer to Guru and thus to God.

Ultimately each person finds his or her own lineage or route through. And when you reach the stage of asking, "God, know me," or "Let me be enlightened," or "I want Nirvana," or however you've said it, at that moment you call forth your spiritual guide or Guru, whom you may not know and may never know until the moment of your enlightenment. That being may be Christ, it may be any one of a number of beings, not necessarily on the physical plane. In fact, for most of us, our real Guru, our Sat Guru, is not on the physical plane. Our Guru will guide us, to the extent that we are asking purely, through one teaching after another. Some of those teachings will be in the form of teachers or situations or experiences. And when we trust that we are in relationship to our Guru, we will constantly learn how to ask our Guru inside, and listen, and tune to the awareness of the presence of our guide, and allow our Guru to guide us, and we will begin to see how each situation is being presented by our Guru to bring us home.

Our Guru or guide represents a unique and specific lineage. Christ represents a lineage. Padmasambhava represents a lineage. Mohammed represents a lineage. Abraham represents a lineage. Maharaj-ji represents a lineage. Not all lineages are necessarily identified with any specific religion. Many of the highest beings have incarnated across time and across religions. Others have come down as a lineage within a religious tradition like a line of tulkus in Tibetan Buddhism, or a line of gurus within Hinduism, rabbis within Judaism, monastic lines within Christianity. Just as Luke is different from John, is different from Paul, is different from Peter, so Milarepa is different from Tilopa. Yellow Cloud is different from Cochise in the Native American tradition. The different Tzaddiks in the mystic tradition of Judaism each represent different lineages. We may ultimately make it through on a specific lineage. We may not have a guide in form, we might be advait, meaning nondualistic, the formless, which would attract us to perhaps Zen Buddhism or Jnana Yoga. Ultimately, we start to fall into a lineage, not because it's the hip thing to do, not because our intellect tells us it's interesting, not because it's a nice community and we like the way they dress, but because that way pulls us and it's our way through.

As we tune to that lineage, our perception shifts, and we begin to notice changes in the figure/ground relationship. We notice teachers we never noticed before; we notice people to be with we never noticed before. The whole process starts to narrow in perceptually, and we start to go directly on what the theosophists call a "ray" coming from God. Even working devotionally with the concept of God is a ray, because merging into God takes you beyond the concept of God. But to know that all ways lead to the end does not nullify the requirement that, sooner or later, we will have to make some sort of commitment or other. A process of surrender is required.

And we go through the lineage. A lineage that is pure is one that catapults us ultimately out the other end; it isn't designed to make us followers of the lineage. It is designed to take us through itself and free us at the other end. A less pure teaching of a lineage traps us in the lineage, makes us a Buddhist or a Christian or a Hindu, not a free being, because when the people who lead do not have the full connection, they cling to the vehicle rather than to the truth toward which the vehicle is directed, and vehicles (institutions) corrode unless they are constantly fed by the living spirit. And the living spirit comes only through beings who *are* it. We can become organizational groupies as part of our path, but if we know it's not enough, we must have the honesty to let it go. Ultimately we will come out of a lineage at the other end and acknowledge that through the Sufi, through the Hebrew, through the Christian, through the Buddhist, through the Hindu, through the Zoroastrian, through lineage after lineage, have come beings who are the living spirit.

Then, like Ramakrishna, we may put on each of the hats, not out of need, but out of acknowledgment, to appreciate the universality of ways. A perfected being is someone who is a state-ment of the culmination of all ways, even though the form in which he or she manifests may be a vehicle for the transmission of a certain lineage. Ramakrishna followed the path of devotion to the Mother. But when he had completed his work, though he remained in the path of devotion to the Mother, he was totally in the advait, nondual state. So at the beginning is eclecticism, at the end is universality, and in the middle is the lineage.

Chapter 8

Guided Meditation

To be read aloud to a spiritual friend as a guided meditation.

Sit straight, so your head, neck, and chest are in a straight line. Start by focusing in your heart area, in the middle of your chest where the Hridayam, the spiritual heart, is located. With your mouth closed, breathe in and out of your chest, focusing on your heart as if you were breathing in and out through your heart. Breathe deeply.

Imagine a substance, a golden mist that fills the air. With every breath, imagine you are pulling into yourself this golden substance. Fill with it; let it pour through your entire body.

Breathe in the energy of the universe. Breathe in the breath of God. Let it fill your whole body. Each time you breathe out, breathe out all of the things in you that keep you from knowing your true self, breathe out all of the separateness, all of the feelings of unworthiness, all the self-pity, all the attachment to your pain, whether it's physical or psychological. Breathe out anger and doubt and greed and lust and confusion. Breathe in God's breath, and breathe out all of the impediments that keep you from knowing God. Let the breath be the transformation.

Now let the golden mist that has poured into your being focus in the middle of your chest; let it take form as a tiny being, the size of a thumb, sitting on a lotus flower right in the middle of your heart. Notice its equanimity, the radiance that makes it bright with a light that comes from within. Use your imagination. And as you look upon this being, become aware that it is radiating light. See the light pouring out of its every pore. As you meditate upon it, experience the deep peace that is emanating from this being. Feel, as you look upon this being, that it is a being of great wisdom. It's sitting quietly, silently, perfectly poised. Feel its compassion and its love. Let yourself be filled with its love.

Now slowly let that tiny being grow in size until it has filled your body so its head just fills the space of your head; its torso, your torso; its arms, your arms; its legs, your legs. So that now in the skin of your body sits this being, a being of infinite wisdom, a being of the deepest compassion, a being who is bathed in bliss, self-effulgent bliss, a being of light, of perfect tranquility. Let this being in your skin begin to grow in size. Experience yourself growing until your head reaches the top of the ceiling and you are sitting beneath the floor and all of the beings gathered within this room are within your body. All of the sounds, even the sound of my voice, are coming from inside you. Feel your vastness, your peace, your equanimity.

Continue to grow. Your head goes up into the sky, blueness all about, until all of your town, your environment, is within you. Look inside and experience the human condition, see the loneliness, the joy, the caring, the violence, the paranoia, the love of a mother for her child, sickness, fear of death, see it all. Realize that it is all within you. Look upon it with compassion, with caring. At the same moment with equanimity, feel the light pouring through your being, inward and outward.

Now grow still larger, feel your vastness increasing until your head is among the planets and you are sitting in the middle of this galaxy, the earth lying deep within your belly. All of humankind lies within you. Feel the turmoil and the longing. Feel the beauty. Sit in this universe, silent, huge, peaceful, compassionate, loving. Let all of the creations of human beings' minds be within you; look upon them with compassion.

Continue to grow until not only this galaxy but every galaxy is within you, until everything you can conceive of is within you. All of it inside you. You are the only one. Feel your aloneness, your silence, your peace. No other beings here, all of the planes of consciousness are within you.

You are the Ancient One. Everything that ever was, is, or will be is part of the dance of your being. You are all of the universe, and so you have Infinite Wisdom; you appreciate all of the feelings of the universe, so you have Infinite Compassion. Let the boundaries of your being disintegrate now and merge yourself into that which is beyond form, and sit for a moment in the formless, beyond time and space, beyond compassion, beyond love, beyond God. . . . Let it all be, perfectly.

Now very gently, very slowly, let the form of the boundaries of your vast being, the One, be reestablished. You are vast, you are silent, and all is within you. Come back from beyond the One and slowly come down in size, come down through the universes into this universe, until your head is once again among the planets and the earth is within you, until your head is once again in the heavens and the cities are within you.

Come down in size until your head is at the top of this room. Stop here for a moment. From this place, look down into the room and find the being who you thought you were when you began this meditation. Look at that being, bringing to bear all of your love and compassion. See the journey of that being as it is living out this incarnation; see its plight, its fears, its doubts, its connection. See all the things it clings to that keep it from being free. See how close it is to knowing who it is. Look within that being and see the purity of its soul.

At this moment reach down from your vast height and very gently, very delicately, with your mind, place your hand very gently on the head of this being, and bestow upon it your blessing, a blessing that in this very life, it may fully know itself. At this moment you are that which blesses and that which is being blessed. Experience both simultaneously.

Come down in size now until you are back into the body which you thought you were when you began. You are still flesh surrounding a being of radiance, of wisdom that comes from being that vast One, of the compassion that comes from being in tune with the truth, and of a love for all things. Feel the love and peace pouring out of you. Use the light that is coming through you now for transmitting that energy, that blessing, to all beings everywhere. Become a lighthouse and send peace and love to all those who suffer.

Think of all the people for whom you have felt less than love. Look to their souls and surround them with light, with love and peace at this moment. Let go of the anger and the judgment.

And then send the light of love and peace out to people who are ill, who are lonely, who are afraid, who have lost their way. Share your blessings, because only when you give can you continue to receive. And you will find that no matter how much you give, you will receive tenfold. As you go on this spiritual journey, you must accept the responsibility to share what you receive, for that is part of the harmony of God, that you become an instrument for the manifestation of the will of God.

Now let the radiant perfect being once again assume its diminutive form, the size of a thumb, sitting upon a lotus flower in your heart, in your spiritual heart in the middle of your chest, radiant with light, peaceful, immensely compassionate. This being is love; this being is wisdom. This is the inner Guru; this is the being within you who always knows. This is the being whom you meet through your deeper and deeper intuition when you've gone beyond your mind. This is the being who is the flow of the universe, the tiny form of the entire universe that exists within you. At any time, you need only sit and quiet your mind and you will hear this being guiding you home. When you have finished the journey, you will have disappeared into this being, surrendered, merged; and then you will recognize that God, the Guru, and the Self are one.

Chapter 9

Dying: An Opportunity for Awakening

Some years ago, as my mother who was dying of cancer got closer to death, I spent quite a bit of time with her. Because I was starting to be into meditation and using psychedelics, I found that I was not particularly anxious about this death, even though my love was very strong. As I would sit in the hospital, often high on one chemical or another, I would watch the parade of people coming into my mother's room—the doctors, the nurses, my relatives, my father—all with a total bravado: "You're looking better today." "Did you eat your soup?" "You'll be up and around in a few days." "The doctor says there is a new medicine." Then they would go out in the hall and say, "She won't last a week."

I saw that she was surrounded by a ring of complete, well-meaning hypocrisy, but all I would do was sit next to her very quietly and sometimes just hold her hand for long periods. One day in the darkening room about a week before she died, she said to me, "You know, I know I'm going to die. I wish I had jumped out a window when I had the strength to do it." Then she said, "There's nobody else I can talk to about it but you." Until then, she and I had never had a conversation about any of this. She said, "What do you think death is?"

I said, "Well, I don't know, but when I look at you, it's like I see somebody I love, a very dear friend, inside a building that's burning. I see the building being destroyed, but somehow, as you and I talk, you and I are still here, and I have the suspicion that even though the body is being consumed by this illness, not much is going to happen." We stayed there in the silence together, just holding hands, for many hours.

It may be relevant to relate two things about the funeral. For forty-four years, my mother and father on their anniversary had exchanged, along with gifts, one red rose that was a token of their love for one another. At the temple the casket was covered with a blanket of roses. As the casket was wheeled out of the temple, it came by the first pew. In the first pew were seated my father, who at the time was a mid-sixties, Boston Republican lawyer, ex-president of a railroad, and very conservative; my oldest brother, a stockbroker-lawyer; my middle brother, also a lawyer, but one who was having spiritual experiences; me; and my sisters-in-law. As the coffin went by the first pew, one rose from the blanket of roses fell at the feet of my father. All of us in the pew looked at the rose. We all knew the story about the exchange of one rose, but of course nobody said anything. As we left the pew, my father picked up the rose and was holding it as we sat in the limousine. Finally, my brother said, "She sent you a last message," and everybody in the car at that moment agreed. Everybody said, "Yes!" The emotions of the moment sanctioned an acceptance of a reality totally alien to at least three members of the group.

Of course, then the question was, how would we preserve the rose? It turned out that my uncle knew someone who had a process where you could put a flower in a liquid and encase it in glass and it would last forever. So the rose was put in this container and placed on the mantelpiece as the final material hold on my mother. A few years later, after a proper period of mourning, my father took a new wife, a very lovely woman. The process of preservation of the rose, however, hadn't been quite perfected, and the color had gone out of the rose into the water, so now it was a ball full of brackish water in which there was a dead flower. There was my mother's message sitting there. It was put in the back of the garage in a cabinet for memorabilia that we can't bear to part with. I'm sure you all have a place like that.

The other part was that I took LSD to go to the funeral, and it was quite interesting because I experienced Mother and me hanging out watching the whole scene. She didn't seem particularly upset, nor was I. The family was seated on one side, and the rest of the people on the other, so that they could watch the family mourn. I was at the end of the row. It was a sunny day, and there was golden light coming out of the casket. Mother and I were hanging out watching all the people who were thinking beautiful thoughts about her. I wanted to smile, but I realized that would be the final straw: "Of course, he takes drugs—he smiles at his own mother's funeral!" A smile is not currently an acceptable social response at the time of somebody's death.

A few years later, prior to meeting Maharaj-ji, I visited the city of Benares, also called Varanasi or Kashi. It is a very sacred city in India. At the time, I knew nothing about Hindu religion or mythology. On the streets in Benares were beings who were just at the point of death. Many were lepers. They would sit in long lines with their begging bowls around the burning ghat. The burning ghat is a platform that goes out into the Ganges River, where all day and all night, one entire caste of people just keeps the fires going in which bodies are cremated. When a person dies in the vicinity, the body is brought through the streets on a stretcher wrapped in cloth, either carried by chanting men or put in a bicycle rickshaw. When the body is taken from the home, it is taken with the head toward the home and the feet toward the Ganges. The recitation on the way is, "Ram Nam Satya Hai, Satya Bol, Satya Hai . . . God's name is Truth." Halfway to the ghat, a ceremony is performed, and the body is turned around so that the head is toward the Ganges, because its home is now beyond form.

Each of the nearly dead beggars on the streets had attached to his loincloth a little bag, which I learned contained enough money for the wood needed for his funeral pyre. At that time the poverty in India deeply frightened me. Their predicament seemed so horrendous to me that I could hardly bear it.

Five months following, when I returned to Benares after having lived in a temple and having begun to understand what Benares was about, I walked through the streets and saw an entirely different scene. Because, as it turns out, Benares is one of the most sacred cities in India, and to die in Benares is the highest desire of the truly spiritual Hindu. It assures liberation; it's a way in which you consciously go toward your death. When you are on your funeral pyre being burned, Shiva, one of the forms of God, whispers the name of Ram, another form of God, in your ear, and you are liberated. So these beings who before had looked so pathetic to me were the ones who had made it; out of all the millions of people in India, these were the ones who had gotten to Benares, who were going to die in Benares and be liberated.

When I looked at them with this knowledge, what I saw on their faces as they looked at me was pity. They were looking at me with pity because I was this foreigner who would probably never die in Benares. I was just caught on the wheel of illusion and suffering, going on and on, while they had made it. I did a complete about-face and began to see that Benares was a city of incredible joy, *even though* it held incredible physical suffering.

So here I am in this old decaying body. It's the package in which I am functioning. I honor it. I take pretty good care of it. Yet, whatever the catalyst, whether it was Maharaj-ji, or psychedelics, or my studies, or meditative experiences, the importance of my body and personality, of the Ram Dass melodrama, have been appreciably lessening. Simultaneously, my anxiety about death has concomitantly been dissipating, and this new perspective has allowed me to reflect upon death and to write about it. Of course, I was deeply influenced by studies of *The Tibetan Book of the Dead,* by Aldous Huxley's description of dying in the book *Island* and by his death, and by my mother's death as well, but it was apparent that we needed new ways of looking at death.

A number of other experiences contributed further to my appreciation of the matter of death, including two Maharaj-ji stories that affected me strongly: One day Maharaj-ji was walking with a devotee of many years, and Maharaj-ji suddenly looked up and said, "Ma just died." She lived in a distant city, and it was obvious he had seen this on another plane. Then he laughed and laughed. His devotee was shocked and called Maharaj-ji a "butcher" for laughing at the death of such a beautiful and pure woman. Maharaj-ji turned and said, "What would you have me do, act like one of the puppets?"

Another time, as Maharaj-ji was sitting with a group of devotees, he suddenly looked around and said, "Somebody's coming," but nobody heard anyone. A few minutes later, an employee of one of Maharaj-ji's devotees arrived. Before he could say anything, Maharaj-ji yelled, "Yes, I know he's dying, but I won't come." The man was shaken by these words because his employer had, just a few minutes before, suffered a severe heart attack and had sent this man running to fetch Maharaj-ji to his side. But no matter how the employee or others pressed Maharaj-ji, he refused to go. Finally Maharaj-ji took a banana and gave it to the employee and said, "Here, take this to him. He'll be all right." Of course the man rushed back with the banana, and the anxious family mashed it up and fed it to the sick man. Just as he finished the banana, he died.

Here in America, Wavy Gravy called me one day and said, "There is a fellow dying who would be interested in visiting with you." I met the boy, who was in his twenties, extremely thin, dressed in Levi pants and jacket, and boots.

I sat down with him and said, "I hear you're going to die soon."

"Yeah," he replied.

I asked him if he wanted to talk about it, and he said okay. We began to talk, and after about twenty minutes, when he went to light a cigarette, I noticed that his hand was shaking; it hadn't been before. Because of my own paranoia, I thought, *Oh, look what I'm doing. What right do I have to be coming on to him? He's the one who's dying.* So I said to him, "Hey, I'm really sorry. I don't mean to upset you, I'll leave you alone. I didn't mean to bug you."

He said, "Oh, no, you're not! I'm nervous because I'm so excited about being with you. I've been looking for the strength to die, and you are the first person I have been around who isn't making it worse by being freaked about it." He was giving me the legitimacy that I didn't have myself; he was saying, "It's okay to do what you're doing."

So we started to hang out together, and at one point I rented a car, and we went for a ride on Highway 1 in Marin County, a very perilous highway along the coast. We stopped for gas, and he said, "Would you mind if I drive? It will probably be the last time." Now that's a pretty romantic image if you know how twenty-three year olds are about driving, so I said, "Sure." He started to drive, but it very quickly became apparent that he was too weak to turn the steering wheel. We were only going about twenty miles an hour, but he would come around one of the curves where there was a three-hundred-foot drop to the ocean, and I would hold the wheel and turn it, trying to do it unobtrusively so that there would be no social blunder; I didn't want to upset him.

As if the situation weren't bad enough at that point, he tried to light a cigarette. I thought, *He's not only going to go, but he's also going to take me with him!* Then I saw that I had entered into a conspiracy—I was joining with him to make-believe he was other than he was, in order to protect his image of himself as this young, virile, twenty-three-year-old. I said to him, "You know, you've got me caught in a conspiracy, because obviously you can't turn the wheel, let alone smoke at the same time. I should be driving. We should be into where it *is,* not where we wish it were. This is the way it is now; let's get here." That remark began a new dialogue between us that got much more exciting, and we just lived in the present moment more and more.

The only preparation for death, it turns out, is the moment-to-moment life process. When you live in the present now, and then this present, and then *this* present, when the moment of death comes, you are not living in the future or in the past. The freaky thing about death is the anticipatory fear of it. But you can't tell someone else to live in the present moment unless you yourself are.

Later I was invited to work with a lawyer who had cancer, and I said, "I only work with people if they want to work with me." I was assured, "Oh, yes, he wants to work with you." So I went out to his place, which was a very posh house by the ocean. He was sitting there surrounded by his family and friends, and they were all drinking. He was ruling the whole scene with an iron hand because he was the one who was dying. They offered me a drink, and I sat looking at the ocean for a bit. I heard hysteria in the conversation, the kind in which everyone is laughing too loudly. Finally, I turned to him and said, "I understand you are going to die soon."

If he had not invited me to come to deal with death, I would have had no license to say such a thing. You can't go up to some-body and say, "I hear you're going to die." You have no license to lay your trip on somebody else, but he had invited me to do what I was doing—it was the compassionate thing to do. The whole place freaked. I had said the thing that nobody ever says, and it entirely changed the space. Then the family and friends, and he and I all got into a discussion of death, sitting by the ocean that beautiful day. We meditated on the ocean, and the whole thing started to take on the power of the immediacy and exquisiteness of the oceanic dying process.

Somewhat later a very dear friend was dying in Los Angeles, and I went to visit her. She was a very subtle, intellectual, liberal, sensitive person. The first time I saw her, she was at the stage where she was interested in death and wanted to talk about it. As I talked, I could hear that intellectual place in her that had not had any experience with reincarnation saying, "I'll listen to it, but it's hogwash." I saw my words were just not doing it.

The next time I went to visit her, she was so weak that all I could do was sit by her bedside. She was dying of cancer of the nervous system, and the pain was very severe in her lower abdomen and groin. While I was sitting there, she was literally writhing in pain, turning her head and rubbing her hands over her body. Her expression was one of intense pain. I was sitting next to her doing the Buddhist meditation on the decaying body. This is a formal meditation that one does on the stages of decay of the human body. I was just sitting there, wide-open, not closing my eyes and going off to some other place, just staying with it, noticing the pain, noticing the whole thing, letting my emotions flow but not clinging, not holding or getting into a judgment about it—just noticing the laws of the universe unfold, which is not easy to do with death, because of our emotional attachment, especially with someone we personally love.

As I sat there watching the pain and suffering, I started to experience a great, deep calm. The room became luminous. And at that moment, right in the midst of her writhing, she turned to me and whispered, "I feel so peaceful." Though her body was writhing with pain, in this meditative environment, she had been able to move beyond the pain and experience deep peace. I, or we, had created this vibrational space that we could be in together. She and I wouldn't have preferred to be in any other place in the universe at that moment. It was bliss.

At a seminar on death and dying guided by Elisabeth Kübler-Ross, a twenty-eight-year-old nurse and mother of four was dying of cancer. She had been through eleven operations, and she asked those of us in attendance, "How would you feel if you came into a hospital room to visit a twenty-eight-year-old mother dying of cancer?" The answers called out from the audience included: anger, frustration, pity, sadness, horror, and confusion. Then she asked us, "How would you feel if you were that twenty-eight-year-old mother and everyone who came to visit felt those feelings?" Suddenly it was apparent to all of us how we surround such a being with our reactions to death and forget that there is a being just like us in that body who needs to make straight contact with someone. It is not unlike the previous point made about the beautiful girl who nobody can relate to other than as a body.

Eric Kast, who did work with LSD in terminal cancer patients, reported on a nurse who was dying of cancer. She took LSD, and it was reported in the *World Medical News* that she said, "I know that I'm dying of this disease, but look at the beauty of the universe." Even though she was busy dying, she also—for a moment—transcended the dying to come into this other place.

Some years ago, Deborah Matthiessen died in Mount Sinai Hospital in New York. Debbie was affiliated with the Zen Center in New York, and when she was dying, the brother monks and students decided that instead of meditating at the zendo, they would come to her hospital room to meditate every night.

The first night, the doctors arrived on their rounds and pushed open the door with their jovial, "How you doin' tonight?" There were all these beings in black sitting deep in meditation, and the doctors were taken aback. As the nights passed, the doctors would come into the room as if coming into a temple, which indeed it was, right in the middle of Mount Sinai Hospital. In the midst of the hospital, the Temple of Life, there it was—a temple to that which is beyond life and death.

In Japan when a person is dying, a screen is placed at the foot of the bed showing the Pure Land of the Buddha. He can focus on that screen, so that as death occurs, the last thoughts are about reaching out. It's like a railway ticket—it's the ticket that is going to take you through, and you can go out on it if you wish.

These various experiences led me more and more to the idea of a center for dying. This was not original to me, but came from Aldous Huxley. It would be a place where people could come to die consciously, surrounded by other beings who were not freaked by death. I thought it should be near the mountains or the ocean, which obviously have eternality connected with them. Perhaps it would have bungalows, and a person could die there in whatever metaphor he or she wanted: as a Christian or a Jew or a Hindu or an atheist. Those coming to die consciously could die with as much or as little medical aid as they wanted. That would be up to them. While they couldn't ask the doctor to kill them, they needn't have their lives prolonged. What would be added, in addition to the priest and medical staff, would be a guide to help the individual remain conscious and in the present.

As I reflected on the term *guide,* it struck me that there are no professional die-ers. Every dying person with whom I shared time helped me probably more than I helped them. Nowadays many people contact me and say, "Do you think I could work with somebody who is dying?" And I see that from each individual's point of view, in terms of his or her own growth, one of the most profound experiences any of us can have is to work with the dying process, whether our own or someone else's. It confronts us with a number of issues in ourselves that are important in our own spiritual growth and awakening. Thus I conceive of the "guide" role as a training role. For, in truth, the guide and the dying person come together to use one another for their own work on themselves. It is a truly collaborative dance between two people.

The abstract point of this is that we don't do anything to anybody else, anyway. Actually, people do things to themselves, and we are merely the environment in which they do it when they are ready. Thus the "guides" must be at a certain stage of their own evolution in order to be environments for awakening through death. They must have a connection with planes of consciousness beyond time and space that lead them to have a philosophical foundation that allows them to be balanced and without panic in the face of death. They must view death not as an end point, but as a process of transformation.

At the level where there is only one of us, it can get scary, because that's where we are confronted with the cessation of ourselves as separate entities. Spiritual practices such as meditation slowly help us to extricate ourselves from attachment to the levels of illusion of our separateness. Until we are free of that illusion and can merge into the ocean of existence without fear, everything we do subtly perpetuates the illusion of separateness. As long as we're attached to our separateness, we can't help but perpetuate fear, because there is a subtle fear in us of losing our separate identity. Because most of us have not fully realized our unity with the cosmos, we must continue to work on ourselves and also continue to serve our fellow sentient beings to relieve suffering. Yet how can we remove suffering when we ourselves still fear? It is a matter of degree. We do what we can for others and yet never stop working on ourselves, for we keep in mind that it is our consciousness that may help to liberate another.

At one point, as I was about to seek funding for a center for dying, Stewart Brand of the *Whole Earth Software Catalog* and *CoEvolution Quarterly,* who is also interested in this field, asked, "Why do you need a center? Why don't you just start with a telephone?" Sort of "Dial-a-Death!" This would allow people to call and ask for help in dealing with their own death. Guides and other assistance would be provided them in their own homes or at hospitals or wherever. We want to bring death out of the hospital environment, as has happened with birth. Or at least, help to create hospital environments that enable you to die consciously.

It was at this point that Stephen Levine, whom I had known as editor of the *Oracle* and a poet in the Haight-Ashbury during the mid-sixties, reappeared in my life. We shared a commitment to meditation and an interest in working with dying. So Stephen and I began to teach together, and soon the Dying Project came into existence with Stephen at the helm. With his wife, Ondrea, he tended a dying hotline in their home and started to lead retreats focused on working consciously and meditatively with death. Out of this work came a remarkable book, *Who Dies?*, followed soon after by *Meetings at the Edge*.

In the early eighties, Dale Borglum joined the project and created the Dying Center in Santa Fe, New Mexico. Here, in a modest way, it was finally possible to explore the concrete manifestation of this dream of a group attempting to live consciously together around the process of dying. This particular experiment lasted about five years. Dale continues to run a much expanded program, the Living/Dying Project, in Marin County.

As we bring death out from under wraps—as we are doing with birth—we become stronger people for our ability to live with the truth of nature. But *compassionate* use of truth requires discretion. In dealing with death, we must be prepared to speak the truth when someone asks us for truth. By the same token, we must remain silent when somebody is trying to deny his or her impending death.

Before my father died he spent a great deal of time worrying about death, because he had gone beyond the actuarial chart point, although he was still quite healthy. In the early 1970s, when I gave seminars about dying out on the lawn of his home with a couple hundred people in attendance, he'd come out and listen for a few minutes and then go back in and watch the ball game. When I went in later, he'd say, "Had a big crowd today." He was just not going to hear it. I would have liked to be able to say to him, "Let me share with you something that will relieve your anxiety, because you're my father and I love you." But, in another sense, we were just two beings who happened to be in an incarnation this time around where he was my father and I was his son, and our approaches to life were very different. I used to bother him about it, but then I stopped. My compassion had ripened a bit, and I could just love him as he was—in his perfection.

Later he asked several times about death and meditation. And once at dinner he said, "Because of our conversations, I don't seem to be as concerned about death as I used to be. I find at times, I'm almost looking forward to it." I took care of him as he approached death and it was the softest and most loving time we had together.

There is a book titled *Life After Life* by Raymond Moody. The book concerns one hundred fifty cases of individuals who were pronounced clinically dead and then were revived—some at accident scenes, some in hospital operating rooms. Many of them reported that during the time they were supposedly dead, they had experiences of floating, reviewing their lives, meeting friends or relatives who had previously died, and meeting a being of light. The power of these data is in the similarities of their reported experiences. Studies of this type are a significant step in bringing life after death into the purview of the Western mind and thus dissipating anxiety about death.

Part of becoming conscious is not trying to impose a limited rational model on how the world is but rather realizing that the rational model is a finite subsystem and that the law of the universe is infinite. To work with someone who is dying is to see the perfection of the dying and at the same moment to work full-time to relieve the suffering involved and to prepare the person for the moment of death.

In the Eastern tradition, the state of your consciousness at the last moment of life is so crucial that you spend your whole life preparing for that moment. We've had many assassinations in our culture, and we wonder what it was like for Bobby Kennedy or Jack Kennedy—if they had any thought, and what those thoughts might have been. *Oh, I've been shot!* or *He did it,* or *Goodbye,* or *Get him,* or *Forgive him.* Mahatma Gandhi walked out into a garden to give a press conference when a gunman shot him three or four times, but as he was falling, the only thing that came out of his mouth was, "Rām. . . ." The name of God. He was ready!

At the moment of death, if we let go lightly, we go out into the light, toward the One, toward God. The only thing that died, after all, was another set of thoughts of who we were this time around.

Chapter 10

Freeing the Mind

Now we're beginning to get a sense of the totality of the sadhana, the practice. We are working with the heart to open a flow with forms in the universe, including thoughts and emotions. That flow ultimately takes everything in form and converts it back into energy. We offer up stuff into the flow to get rid of it.

The offering up or the cleaning is called purification. It exists in every religion. In Raja Yoga these are the yamas, or it's the various vows we take in Buddhism, or the abstinences and commandments in Christianity and Judaism. These are done out of what is called "discriminative awareness." That is, we understand that we are entities passing through a life in which the entire life drama is a curriculum for our awakening. We see that the life experience is a vehicle for coming to God, for becoming conscious, for becoming liberated. And we understand that ultimately that's what we're doing here.

When we're really wanting God, not just wanting to want God, we understand that is all we are doing here. When we are only wanting to want God, we say, "Well, I have this and that to do, but I'd like to live my life in order to return to God." If we have studied the Four Noble Truths of Buddha, we've come to understand that the liberation from clinging and attachment is the liberation from suffering, and that liberates all beings from suffering. Or if we are thinking, *Well, I can't just want to go to God; I must help other human beings as well,* we begin to see that these are not polarized, that these are very intimately integrated. Because every act we perform for other human beings can liberate them to the extent that we are liberated. If we feed someone with attachment, we fill his belly, but we also reinforce his attachments. And that reinforcement perpetuates his long-term suffering. Thus, ultimately, we understand that every act we do in life becomes an act of work on ourselves—because that is the highest thing we can do for all sentient beings, whether we're feeding somebody, or sitting in a cave meditating, or making people laugh, or providing a service or goods, or making a sandal. Whatever we're doing, we're a transmission of our being.

For instance, the image we have of musicians is of entertainers: someone playing music for other people to hear. As we begin more clearly to hear what the dance is about, we understand we are souls on the journey toward our own liberation, and everything is grist for the mill, including our flutes and our flute-playing. Then we are doing what the *Bhagavad Gita* talks about; we are playing the flute as an offering to God. So we're playing it back into the circle. And as we use the flute-playing as an act of purification, it's no longer "my" flute, and it's not played for ego gratification. It's part of sadhana; it's an offering—the whole process is an offering. Then the flute-playing starts to get pure and come from a higher and higher space.

If we listen to, for example, Bismillah Khan play the shenai, we hear a being who is playing to God, and that circle is so closed that it's God playing to Itself. Other human beings simply listen in. And because it's played that way, the subtle consciousness of the artist doesn't suck another person into "being entertained." Because the separation between entertainer and entertained is a distinction between subject and object; it's a distance between human beings. When we are part of the instrument of the music of God just playing to Itself, then anyone can tune in and become part of that same circle. And there's only one of it. There's no separation.

The minute we think we're entertaining somebody, the minute we think we're feeding somebody, the minute we think there's a "them" out there, we just lost it. We just stopped the flow. Our concepts stop the flow, because the mind, the thinking mind, works in relation to subject and object. And the minute we think about who somebody else is, the minute we define that person as somebody who needs food, and that's the reality, the only reality, we have made them into an object. No matter how much we feed them, we've still got them separate from us. Most people who give, in America, give out of paranoia and fear—it's like giving to keep people away.

I remember lecturing—I believe in Portland in the civic community center, though usually I lecture in more funky spaces—and there was a big orchestra pit between me and the audience, which was "out there." We couldn't even get the lights up high enough to see the audience. The whole game was designed to make everybody object and subject. There was a great barrier like a moat to protect you from the masses. It was incredible! And the insurance laws didn't allow me to have anybody on stage. I was alone on the stage with Krishna Das—a stage large enough to hold a whole opera company. And there's a sea of "them" out there who have come to be entertained, which is the traditional way of show business. But cutting through that doesn't necessarily demand a change in the physical game. It would have been nice if everybody was sitting around me, close and friendly. But it isn't critical. It's where my head is at. And it's where our heads are at in every act we perform that determines whether that act liberates or entraps us and everybody around us.

Now we're approaching the issue of no-mind. How do we use our thoughts, and how do we transcend them? How do we go beyond mind? When we acknowledge that our lives are vehicles for our liberation, it becomes clear that all of our life experiences are the optimum experience we need in order to awaken. The minute we perceive them that way, they are useful within that domain. The minute we ignore that perception, they won't work that way.

In psychology there's a term *functional fixedness*. You look at a hammer, and you think of a hammer as an instrument to hammer nails. You might need something to serve as a pendulum, but every time you look at the hammer, you only see something to hammer nails. The idea that the hammer could be attached to a string and used as a pendulum doesn't come through, because you can't break the functional fixedness; you've got a set about how it's supposed to be, and you can't break that set.

Well, it's the same thing with life experiences. A culture has a set about what the meaning of experiences is all about—like what death is about or what deviant behavior is about. Is it insanity, or is it mystical wisdom? There are all these models in a culture, all its functional fixedness that we absorb as to what our life experiences are about. Is it gratifying? Is it pleasant or painful? The model this culture works within is a model of gratification through external agents, getting more from the environment, man over nature, control and mastery for gratification, for creating our own personal heaven in which our egos stay paramount, our egos are "God." That's different from a culture such as the Hopi Indians, where we hear about a balance of man and nature, harmony, the Tao, the flow—man *in* nature, rather than man *over* nature. It's not mastery and control; it's listening to hear the way in which we play a part in flow. Then it's not just our personal gratification; it's us being part of a process that transcends our own separateness. That's a way of talking about God. That's God in form.

The models we have in our minds of our experiences determine whether those experiences can liberate us or will continue to entrap us. This is the beginning of the use of the mind. This is discriminative awareness—that is, making the discrimination between those things, or those ways of looking at things, that will bring us close to God, to our own freedom, and those things that will take us away from it.

Now, at the stage that many people I meet are at, they do their practice, their method, as "good" and as well as they can. And then they take a little time off. They say, "Well that's been great; now what do you say we have a pizza and a beer and listen to some good music?" Now that—pizza, beer, and music—could do it for them too, except in their mind there's a model that the "time off" has nothing to do with it. We've got these models in our heads about what's going to get us there. Meditation, we suppose, will get us there—pizza, we presume, will not. But the pizza, beer, and rock music could do it for us if we were open to the flow of it, and the meditation might not if we're busy being righteous about it—because there's no act in and of itself that is either dharmic or adharmic. It's who's doing it and why they're doing it that determines whether it's wholesome or not. To stick a knife in somebody can be adharmic, taking that person away from God, but if you're a surgeon, it could be bringing him to God. Obviously the act of the knife into the person isn't the issue. It's who's doing what, how. Even two surgeons could use that knife differently, one dharmically, the other adharmically; yet both think they're trying to save somebody. One is tuned to God's will, and one is not. One is on an ego trip of "I'll save you," and one is healing in the way of things, and says, "If it be Thy will, O Lord."

The statement, "If it be Thy will, O Lord," is "If it be in the nature of things, if it be in the Natural Law, if it be in the flow of perfection of form." God, or the Natural Law, or the Divine Law, does not have to be judged by us. It has to be understood by us and heard by us and felt by us, and heeded by us.

So we ask ourselves, "How do I use my every moment to get there?" Not heavy, tight, "I've got to be careful; I might make a mistake." Light, dancing, trusting, quieting, flowing. It's got to be done with the flow of love and the quietness of mind. It's like the women in India who go to the well and come back with jugs full of water on their heads. They're talking and gossiping as they walk, but they never forget the jugs of water on their heads. The jug of water is what our journey is all about. In the course of it, we do what we do in life, but we don't forget the jug of water. We don't forget what it's all about. We keep our eye on the mark. At first we have to prime the pump a little bit to do it; and we keep forgetting and remembering and forgetting and remembering. That's what the illusion is. The illusion keeps pulling us back into forgetting. Lost in our melodrama: my love life, my child, my livelihood, my gratification. "Somebody ripped off my stereo," "I don't have a thing to wear," "Am I getting enough sex?" . . . just more and more stuff. And we keep forgetting into it.

And every now and then, we remember. We sit down and meditate, or we read Ramakrishna or Ramana Maharshi and suddenly, "Oh yeah, right; whew! That's what it was about." And we remember again. And then a moment later, we forget. But what happens is the balance shifts. If we can imagine a wheel whose rim is the cycle of births and deaths, all of the "stuff" of life, conditioned reality, and whose center is perfect flow, formless no-mind, the source, we've got one foot with most of our weight on the circumference of the wheel, and one foot tentatively on the center. That's the beginning of awakening. And we come in, and we sit down and meditate, and suddenly there's a moment when we feel the perfection of our being and our connection. And even beyond that, we just are. We're just like a tree or a stream. There's only a second or two of it there at the hub. Then our weight goes back on the outside of the wheel. Over and over and over, this happens. Slowly, slowly the weight shifts. Then the weight shifts just enough so that there is a slight predominance on the center of the wheel, and we find that we naturally just want to sit down and be quiet, that we don't have to say, "I've got to meditate now," or "I've got to read a holy book," or "I've got to turn off the television set," or "I've got to do . . ." anything. It doesn't become that kind of a discipline anymore. The balance has shifted. And we keep allowing our lives to become more and more simple, more and more harmonious. And less and less are we grabbing at this and pushing that away.

We are listening to hear how it is rather than imposing a structure, because we see that if we keep imposing structures, it doesn't get us freer. And we begin to forget our own romantic storyline. "Who am I becoming?" "What will I be when I grow up?" All of these models just fall away. We just start to sit simply, live simply, be where we are, be with whom we're with when we're with them. We hear our dharma. If it's making shoes, we make shoes. And we're making the shoe with our consciousness in the present, simple and easy, not having a fantasy of surfing in Hawaii. We're just making a shoe. And because of the consciousness that we're bringing into that making of a shoe, the no-mind quality of it, it becomes the perfect statement of *shoeness* that can come through us with our skills at that moment.

When we can just make a shoe, *while* we make a shoe, we *are* the meditation. There's nothing to do. Our whole life is a meditative act. There's no time we leave meditation. It's not just sitting on our meditation pillows, our zafus. All of life is a big zafu—no matter whether we're driving or making love. Whatever we're doing, it's all meditation. It becomes interesting to reflect on our life as to which acts can be done from the zafu and which can't. Which acts would fall away were they done from this space of just clear, quiet presence? It's just a natural shedding that occurs as part of the process that we're all in.

Which brings us to an interesting space, dealing with free will and determinism. In truth, I cannot yet fathom this issue fully and clearly. But I will share with you what I thus far can understand. Within the perfection of this divine plan is included the freedom of an individual to choose to be harmonious with, or to go against, the law. The way that was depicted in the Bible was Adam and Eve's choice to eat the apple. *God,* we can say, is the word that describes, that symbolically represents, that Divine Law that says, "Live here in the perfection of the flow, but refrain from eating the apple." But the choice whether we want to eat the apple or not exists within the Garden of Eden as well as everywhere else. The apple represents the separation of the individual from the flow in his own mind—the subject-object, self-conscious reality. That is knowing it rather than being it. Chomp! The eating of the apple. Separation.

As was said before, after the separation, God looks at Adam and Eve, and they're wearing fig leaves over their genitals, and he says, "Who told you that you were naked?" Because if we were one with the flow, why would we have shame or separateness or any of those things? We've all experienced the innocence in which nakedness is just pure flow and beauty. We have all experienced shame. We've been with babies, and we've seen the freedom in that flow. And we all have yearned to have that flow back again. Being the flow is that innocence.

Though the choice is available all along, until the lifetime in which we begin to awaken, we don't identify with anything other than that which is totally determined. Until then, we identify with our thoughts, but our thoughts are all lawfully determined. They are all within the laws of cause and effect. But who we really are is not our thoughts. The "we" that we thought we were turns out to be a conditioned, mechanical process of body and thought, and the "we" who we really are goes back into the Void, the flow, the Dharma itself. The optimum strategy is to act as if we have free choice and to choose always that which we feel is most in harmony with the way of things.

One way of saying it is that before we awaken, we are determined. It is totally God's will. Once we awaken, we are free to choose between man's will and God's will—free to choose to look up or not to look up. That is one way of saying it. For example, we think that we picked up a book out of some kind of free choice. But our interests and economics and intellectual capabilities are all products of certain previous conditions. In fact, there are beings with the ability to get outside of time who can see that this is the choice we would have made, because they can see the way in which the laws work and out of what "stuff" that choice came. In that sense, that was not totally free choice. And yet it's not fatalistic.

The issues of determinism and free will—fatalism, karma, dependent origination—all weave an incredibly complex pattern that I think would be somewhat beyond the scope of this work to explore. So I'm saying that we act as if we are free agents and choose to awaken. In other words, we have real discriminative awareness to use. A skillful use of the intellect is contemplation. For example, every morning, work with a thought. Take a holy book. Don't read pages, don't collect it. Take one thought and just sit with it for about ten or fifteen minutes.

You could contemplate on the qualities of Christ. Charity. Suffering. Every day you contemplate on the stuff you're becoming.

Sri Ramakrishna said, "If you meditate on your ideal, you will acquire its nature. If you think of God day and night, you will acquire the nature of God."

So we fill our minds with things that are going to get us there. Our minds don't have to be filled only with the daily news to prove that we're good citizens. We don't have to be at the mercy of all this, the constant onslaught of media. We could fill our minds instead with the stuff that liberates us—ultimately becoming aware of that which gets us to God and that which doesn't, to help us let go of that which doesn't.

We begin to develop the power of our minds through concentration, through one-pointedness. Following the breath, following the mantra, whatever is our dharmic choice, we develop the capacity to put the mind on one thought and keep it there and let everything else flow by. We don't stop our minds. We let them flow. But we bring one thought constantly to the surface. We keep coming back to one thought all the time. Breathing in, breathing out. Breathing in, breathing out. Rising, falling. We note breathing in, breathing out; or we use our mantra, "Ram, Ram, Ram, Ram, Ram, Ram, Ram, Ram, Ram, Ram." Eating, sleeping, making love . . . "Ram, Ram." We "Ram-ize" it. We convert it all by maintaining a frame of reference. That has the dual capacity of centering us and increasing the power of one-pointedness. A one-pointed mind is free of the intellect. It is a supple, useful mind.

You see, we can use our intellects to judge the universe or to clean up our own games. If we judge the universe, we are using our intellect to take us away from God; if we use it to clean up our own game, it can take us toward God, toward the Tao, the way of things, the Divine Plan as discussed in Judaism, Christianity, Islam, Hinduism, Zoroastrianism. We could call it the Mind of God; we could call it the Natural Law; we could call it the way in which everything in form is related to everything else—that is the flow, and that flow is harmonious in its parts. Even the cacophonous parts are harmonious in the larger scope of things. They are not lawful in a linear, analytic, logical sense. Natural Law includes paradox, which logical law cannot. "A" can be "A" and "not-A" at the same moment. It's not a law that we can grok with our intellect. It's a law that we can become, but we can't know. The closest we come to a sensing of the law is what we in the West call intuitive wisdom. Gurdjieff called it "the higher faculty." It's a higher way of knowing, a subjective involvement in the universe, not an objective one. We don't know the law; we are the law. And we sense, when we have a quiet mind, the way of things.

Just as some Native American tribes would send a pubescent boy out into the wilderness for a few days or weeks to fast and listen, to become quiet, and to attune to the way of things, so it is necessary to get quiet enough to hear not only the singing mating calls of the birds but also the way of our own sexual desires, the way of our own patterns of anger, the way of our own hearts, the way of the decay of our bodies—without getting lost in grabbing hold, in judgment or analysis or clinging or fear, but just hearing it as it is. It's not the objective "witness" in the sense of standing back and looking. It's a subjective being part of it without attachment anywhere. It's a very subtle place I'm talking about now. It's the use of the mind beyond the intellect. The intellect is the first step of it, discriminative awareness—looking around and saying, "This anger isn't going to get me to God. I'm going to drop it." We drop it because we see where we're going this lifetime. It's like we're going to New York City, and we come to a road that leads to Mexico, but we don't take it this time. Mexico is beautiful, but it's not where we're going this time around.

Discriminative awareness is based on goal-oriented behavior. But as we get near the end of the journey, we must give up even the concept of the goal, and of the trying, and of being someone seeking, because even those concepts ultimately keep us back. All concepts, all models, all molds, all programs in our heads, are limiting conditions. No-mind, the sufficient faith to exist in no-mind, to just be empty and trust that as a situation arises, out of us will come what is necessary to deal with that situation—including the use of our intellect where appropriate. Our intellect need not be constantly held on to in order to keep reassuring us that we know where we are, out of fear of loss of control. Ultimately, when we stop identifying so much with our physical bodies and with our psychological entities, that anxiety starts to dissolve. We start to define ourselves as in flow with the universe, and whatever comes along—death, life, joy, sadness—is grist for the mill of awakening. Not "this" versus "that," but "whatever."

Under those conditions we don't have to do so much labeling. We can just be quiet and let the universe happen. But that trust is based on giving up our own unworthiness. Because if we think we need our minds to keep us under control—that if we lost control we would become wild, destructive, chaotic, uncaring, insensitive beings—then we are defining ourselves as Freud did, as totally selfish behavior. But the predicament is, that's defining our existence from just the first two chakras. Even when Adler comes along and says the real guts of the human being is about power, that too is only the third chakra. Beyond that is the fourth heart chakra that harmonizes seeming opposites, and brings it all into flowing understanding and acceptance. And beyond that, we also exist in the fifth, sixth, and seventh chakras as well.

Once we begin to awaken and sense who we are, we begin to understand how we are becoming the Dharma, how as we attune, we literally cannot hurt another human being. We cannot go out and do them in, because not only does our intellect understand the karmic implications of it, but also our perception is such that we see ourselves hurting ourselves. The concept of brotherhood is no longer an intellectual, liberal concept; it's a perceptual reality. Living within that reality, it's impossible to perform certain acts we might have done before. And that's what the Ten Commandments are about. They are a statement of how it is when we see things as they are. But because most exoteric religions are written for people who are not awakened, they've become moral prescriptions, using guilt to control behavior, to move people slowly in that direction.

We must become in our own lives the living statement of the Vedas, of the Commandments, of the Law. A conscious human being *is* the Law, *is* the Dharma. We don't know the Dharma, or recite the Dharma. We are the Dharma. Our every act. The way a roshi washes a dish is the Dharma. That washing of the dish is in perfect harmony with all the forces in the universe at that moment. No mind involved, no analytic thought, *Am I doing the right thing?* In discriminative awareness, the intellect is used only in the early stages. Later, there is no-mind. The intellect is useful as a servant, but not as a master. It is available to do analytic work when we need it. It's as beautiful and powerful an instrument as our prehensile skill, as our ability to oppose thumb and index finger, an ability we're delighted we have. If we didn't have that prehensile ability, it would change our lives considerably. But we don't have to go around all day picking up things just to keep showing we can do it. I mean the awe for it diminishes after a while. It's a power, a siddhi, that we have because of our simian nature. Apes have it too. So too our cerebral cortex is a power, because of our *Homo sapien* nature. We can sit around and flex it, in the *New York Times* or wherever we wish, to the delight of everybody. Fascinated with our own power. Going to the moon is a projection of our human intellect. Man over nature. Though we worship the human intellect, as an exquisite power, it is very trivial in the greater design of the natural law of things.

The question is: are we going to play big league, or do we want to play sandlot ball? That's really what it boils down to. In big league, the intellect is available. I'm no more stupid than I ever was. My mind is perfectly good, as good as it was when I worshipped it as a professor at Harvard. But it's sure not a very big part of my life. And even at this moment, as all this stuff is coming out, I'm enjoying it as much as you are; it's coming out of a place of emptiness in me. I couldn't care less. It's coming out because this situation is eliciting it, because our collective mind is eliciting this kind of clarification of our predicament at this moment. It's dharmically appropriate for this moment. I have no ego investment in this stuff, because it isn't mine. If we don't deviate the flow or color it with our own trips, it comes through purely in whatever form it is our dharma to express, and the mind is freed.

Chapter 11

Nobody's Special

We are in training to be nobody special. And it is in that nobody-specialness that we can be anybody. The fatigue, the neurosis, the anxiety, the fear—all come from identifying with somebodyness. But we have to start somewhere. It does seem that we have to be somebody before we can become nobody. If we started out being nobody at the beginning of this incarnation, we probably wouldn't have made it this far. Blue babies are examples of nobody special; they just don't have the will to breathe or eat or live. For it's that force of somebodyness that develops the social and physical survival mechanisms. It's only now, having evolved to this point, that we learn to put that somebodyness, that whole survival kit, which is called the ego, into perspective.

When I was a Harvard professor, I would spend all my time thinking. I was paid for that. I would have clipboards and tape recorders to collect all my thoughts. Now I'm becoming more and more simple as I quiet. Sometimes there seems to be no one in there at all, and I just sit. Then, when something needs to happen, it happens, even thinking or speaking, and I just witness it.

It's very far out when we begin not to think, or the thinking is going by, and we're not identified with being the thinker. At first we really "think" we've lost something. It's awhile before we can appreciate the peace that comes from the simplicity of no-mind, of just emptiness, of not having to be somebody all the time. We've been somebody long enough. We spent the first half of our lives becoming somebody. Now we can work on becoming nobody, which is really somebody.

For when we become nobody, there is no tension, no pretense, no one trying to be anyone or anything, and the natural state of the mind shines through unobstructed. The natural state of the mind is pure love, which is not other than pure awareness. Can you imagine when we become that place we've only touched through our meditations? When we *are* love? We've finally acknowledged who we really are. We've cleared away all of the mind trips that kept us being who we thought we were. Now, everybody we look at we're in love with. We experience the exquisiteness of being in love with everybody and not having to do anything about it—because we've developed compassion. The compassion is to let people be as they need to be without changing them. The only time we might need to intervene with people is when their actions are limiting the opportunities for other human beings to be free. And then the way in which we intervene is very mindfully and open-heartedly. For if we are busy being somebody trying to change someone, we're just creating more anger. If we are nobody special, but it is our dharma to oppose injustice, then it is merely an act of the Dharma. And not for a moment do we lose that total love for the other person who is not other than us. For being nobody, there is nobody we're not.

Had we sufficient discipline, we could pursue the steepest of paths to get rid of all the ways we cling to models of ourselves. We could just sit—Zen Buddhism—and every thought that comes by that creates another reality, we would let it go. And clinging to none, we would know enlightenment. Or we might pursue the path of Ramana Maharshi—Atma Vicharya, "Who am I?" We simply ask, "Who am I? Who am I?" And slowly we watch ourselves be other than all the ways in which we identify ourselves—as a body, organs, emotions, social roles—we see it all. We keep dissociating from it until we are left with the thought of I. "I am the thought I." This path takes incredible discipline, for as we have freed ourselves from our bodies and our emotions, and we're just about to drop this last thought of I, our bodies grab us again. And we're back in our habitual thoughts about our bodies, our identities.

Most of the time when we watch our mind, we find it keeps grabbing at things and making them the foreground. And everything else becomes the background. When we're reading, we're not listening. When we're listening, we're not seeing. When we're remembering, we forget where we are. But can we function when the world is all background and awareness itself is foreground?

When awareness is identified with thoughts, we only exist in a certain time/space dimension. But when awareness goes behind thought, we are able to be free of time and see thoughts appearing and disappearing, just watching thought forms come into existence, exist, and pass away in a millisecond. And when the intensity of concentration allows us to see the space between two thoughts, we see eternity. There is no thought there. We realize that thoughts exist against the backdrop of no thought. Against the backdrop of emptiness, of nothing, we exist. And there we are at the edge of perceiving who we are. Then we face one of the greatest fears we will ever confront: the fear of our own extinction. The fear of ceasing to exist—not just as a body, but even as a soul. It is similar to the statement made by Huang Po about people approaching this point: that they become fearful to enter into what they consider "the void," distressed that once they let go into it, they will drop unendingly, that there will be nothing to stay their fall, not realizing the Void is the Dharma itself.

But as we're ready for the ultimate mystic doorway, the inner door of the seventh temple, we say, "I am not this thought." We let go of even the great fear of nonexistence. The senses are just working by themselves. There is hearing occurring, but there is no listener. There is seeing, but there is no seer. The senses are just all doing their thing, but there's nobody home. If the mind thinks, *I am aware,* that is recognized as just another thought, a part of the show passing by. It's not awareness itself. Thoughts are going by like a river, and awareness simply is. When we become just awareness, there is no more "me" being aware.

By letting go of even the thought *I,* what is left? There is nowhere to stand and no one to stand there. No separation anywhere. Pure awareness. Neither this, nor that. Just clarity and being.

Chapter 12

Karmuppance

In the mid-sixties there seemed to be an expectation that if we got high, we'd be free. We were not quite realistic about the profundity of man's attachments and deep clingings. We thought that if only we knew how to get high the right way, we wouldn't come down. And that was our attempt. Then in the late sixties, there was the idea that if we joined the movement and became part of a model of how to stay high, we'd be able to do it. So in the late sixties and early seventies, there was a tremendous interest in mass movements.

Now people are realizing that it's somewhat of a long haul. They're feeling transformations in themselves, but they're working with their lows as well as their highs, they're cleaning up their games. And the reason we clean stuff away and don't just get high, why we focus on our depression and our negativity and all of our heavies, is because we're getting hip to the fact that if we push stuff under the rug, sooner or later there is karmuppance.

I was invited to visit "death row" in San Quentin. To be honest, I sat outside the prison before I went in, in my rented car, looking at San Quentin, thinking, *I'll be happy to go in; and I'll be happy to come out*—because there is a certain kind of paranoia in the searching procedures and the authority structure that I have to keep dealing with in myself. I went in and was met by all the yogis who teach there and the acting warden, who was a very nice guy. And we were immediately whisked up to death row. There are actually two rows, because there are so many of these fellows; they are in separate cells, segregated in two long rows separated by a wall.

As I went up to each cell, out of the thirty-four men, there were not more than five who did not receive me openly, clearly, quietly, consciously. The feeling I had was that I was visiting a monastery, and that these were monks in their cells, for these men, who are facing death, have been pushed into a situation that has cut through their melodramas, and they are right here. We sat together in groups of ten, and as part of the meditation, we were sending out thought forms of love and peace to all sentient beings in the universe. I became so affected by the vibration of the space that it was very hard for me to move on to the next group. There was light pouring out of these beings' eyes.

And we got so open that I was able to say, without any of us freaking, "I can't tell whether what's happened to you is a blessing or a curse, for there is very little chance that we would be sharing this high a space, or even would have met, were you not in this situation." To prove my point, I'll tell you that I spent half an hour on one of the other segregated mainline cell blocks. And of these beings, the percentage of those open was just what you'd expect in our society. Maybe one out of a hundred was right there with me. From the rest, you could feel the cynicism, the doubt, the putdown, the sarcasm.

Now, the bizarre humor of all this is that if Supreme Court rulings were to stop the death penalty, these men would all become lifers and almost all of them would lose this consciousness. Yet if they die, they will have this consciousness right up to the moment of execution, which does not mean that all the karma accrued to them—because in most cases, they have been involved in killing another human being—is over, because one can go into death with "Ram" on his lips, with Christ in his heart, high and clear. But whatever stuff is covered over by his situational high at the time of dying, as his ego structure starts to lose its control, the stuff that's left will bubble up again, and he is going to have his karmuppance, he will once again renew his karmic run-through.

There is a story about an old Zen monk who was dying, who had finished everything and was about to get off the wheel. He was just floating away, free and in his pure Buddha-mind, when a thought passed by of a beautiful deer he had once seen in a field. And he held on to that thought for just a second because of its beauty, and immediately he took birth again as a deer. It's as subtle as that.

We can't cheat the game by getting high—that's the point. The situation these fellows are in is forcing their openness and awareness, but it's not totally burning out their karma. It will help. One moment in which they feel compassion for the person they may have murdered will do much for their karma, but it's not going to purify all of it.

It's like when we begin to see the work that is to be done, and we go to an ashram or a monastery, or we hang out with satsang. We surround ourselves with a community of beings who think the way we think. And then none of the stuff, the really hairy stuff inside ourselves, comes up. It all gets pushed underground. We can sit in a temple or a cave in India and get so holy, so clear and radiant, the light is pouring out of us. But when we come out of that cave, when we leave that supportive structure that worked with our strengths but seldom confronted us with our weaknesses, our old habit patterns tend to reappear, and we come back into the same old games, the games we were sure we had finished with. Because there were uncooked seeds, seeds of desires that sprout again the minute they are stimulated. We can stay in very holy places, and the seeds sit there dormant and uncooked. But there is fear in such individuals, because they know they're still vulnerable.

Nothing goes under the rug. We can't hide in our highness any more than we've hidden in our unworthiness. If we have finally decided we want God, we've got to give it all up. The process is one of keeping the ground as we go up, so we always have ground, so that we're high and low at the same moment—that's a tough game to learn, but it's a very important one. So at the same moment that if I could, I would like to take us all up higher and higher, we see that the game isn't to get high—the game is to get balanced and liberated.

Most of us find that the veils of the illusion, of the clinging, are very thick, and we want to do things to burn up these veils, to purify ourselves and get on with it. And even though the whole model of getting on with it and going from here to there is itself a trap, we still can skillfully use that trap to clear away other obstacles that are hindering us. Then, ultimately, we can give up the trap of attachment to the method itself.

We are coming out of a cultural tradition in which, once you saw where you wanted to go, you took the most direct and aggressive path to get there. And impatience is part of the quality of our tradition. It's what made our country great. But the predicament we face is that the beginning of this awakening often comes long before we are really ready to let go of all the ways in which we cling. Some of these methods just become very powerful means of up-leveling old games, of reinforcing heavy ego trips. I know people who've meditated for years who wear their methods like merit badges. "I've done six Vipassana courses, three sesshins, and a double dervish. I get up at four every morning. I can sit without moving for hours. My mind goes absolutely blank." They're professional meditators. They have, to some degree, mastered their method, but they have not loosened the hold of grasping and greed. Their method has just become another form of worldliness. Nothing much is happening, because it's such an ego trip. There are, for instance, people who can go into samadhi and stay there for long periods, but when they come back, they're no wiser than when they entered that state.

It's like the story of the king who promised a yogi the best horse in the kingdom if he could go into deep samadhi and be buried alive for a year. So they buried the yogi, but in the course of the year, the kingdom was overthrown, and nobody remembered to dig up the yogi. About ten years later, someone came across the yogi still in his deep trance and whispered, "Om," in his ear, and he was roused. And the first thing he said was, "Where's my horse?"

Spiritual work can be like gambling on a game of roulette. You put your money down, and the ball goes around and drops

124 Grist for the Mill

into the slot your money was on. And they say, "Do you want to take your money or let it ride?" Anywhere on this journey, we can take our money and pull out and go spend it. Or we can let it ride. Do we want to just double our money, or do we want to go for broke? Do we just want a little social leverage, or do we want to get done? It's no different than Mara confronting Buddha as he sits under the bodhi tree, for as we get closer to the inner gates of freedom, of enlightenment, of liberation, the subtle clingings will be fanned all the more, and the opportunities for gratification keep increasing. Because of the one-pointedness developed through meditation, we become able to cut through our own limits of consciousness and see some of what it's all about. But if we have power needs, we are then all too ready to use what we see to have power over other beings. If our spiritual work has come out of wisdom, not out of a need for power but out of a yearning for God, then when the powers come, we just notice them, realizing they are going to take us on tangents, consume them, and keep going. We just have to trust the light and let our money ride. For as long as we think we are "somebody," we aren't yet quiet enough to be in tune with all of it, and thus any action taken is done from our own particular separate perspective.

As long as we are in an incarnation, there will be action. As long as there is form, there will be change. But it depends on who is doing the acting or who thinks acting is being done that will determine whether that act is part of the flow of things or antagonistic to it. It's like the story about the prince's butcher. The prince asked the butcher how, although he had been cutting with the same knife for nineteen years, it never needed to be sharpened. And the butcher explained that he is in tune with what he is cutting, that the knife finds its own way into the joint, above the bone, through the muscle, that it doesn't hit against the joint, that it just finds its way around the bone. Because he is tuned, he is what he is doing. He isn't busy being a butcher cutting a piece of meat—he is awareness, and that awareness includes the meat and the butcher and the knife. There is an act happening, but there is no doer of the act because there's nobody who thinks he's a butcher.

When we are in harmony with the way everything proceeds from everything else, we cannot act wrongly. For not only are we in tune with the particular act we are doing in terms of time, but with all of the ways in which that act is interrelated with everything in the universe. It is a level of awareness from which actions are manifested that have no clinging—not even clinging to the effects of the act. We are not holding on anywhere. We're right here, always in the new existential moment. Moment to moment, it's a new mind. No personal history. We just keep giving up our storylines.

Each person gets his karmuppance. If we focus on God, we get God. If we want power, we get power. If we want more of something, we get it. The horror is that we get everything we want—sooner or later, if not in this incarnation, then another. And often when we finally get it, we don't want it. The process of karmic fruition speeds up, because, as we get closer, we see ourselves living out old karma, old desires. As our life gets freer and freer of attachments, we create less and less karma, for karma is created by an act done with attachment. When we're not clinging to senses or to thoughts, we are not creating more karma. There is no one intending anything to happen in any way; there is no

one separate to act in a separate way. When there is no attachment or identification with thoughts and feelings, there is no
reactive push into action creating more doing, more karma. Not
identifying, not being separate, cooks these seeds and consumes
the grasping for more.

We get to the point where our acts are not done out of attachment but instead are just done as they're done, and no new stuff
is being created. There is just old stuff running off, but nobody
being affected by it because there is nothing in us that clings to
a model of who we are or aren't. It all becomes just passing show.
There is no investment in its representing us as "individuals." It is
just the outcome of previous input, just old conditioning clicking
along, just more grist for the mill.

Chapter 13

Methods and More

We come together, representatives of many forms, many methods. All the way from Krishnamurti, who says there is no method, to Krishna Consciousness or Fundamental Christianity, which say, "Our way is the only way," with defined forms. Where we meet is in what is common to all these forms. And what is common to all of our forms is not another form. What is common to all of our forms is choiceless awareness, is pure love, is flow and harmony in the universe, the absence of clinging, spaciousness. We can call this "Buddha Mind." We can call it "the Heart of Allah." We could call it "Christ consciousness." We could call it "Yahweh," or "G-d." I have involved myself with many forms. Methods of Vipassana meditation, to make me more mindful, to quiet my mind and to bring it to one-pointedness. Devotional practices, worshipping the feet of my Guru, and singing Hare Krishna and Sri Ram Jai Ram. Zen meditation, confronting a koan, or just sitting. Study, of the *Bhagavad Gita,* of *The Tibetan Book of the Great Liberation,* of Chuang Tzu and Lao Tzu. Of the *I Ching* and the *Tao Te Ching,* of the New Testament and the Old Testament, and on and on. How does it all come together? There is no form that represents the amalgam of all those things.

If we follow all these methods to the apex, we are pushed beyond form. We are pushed into the moment. The merging with God is right here.

Be right here, aware of sitting here, aware of the self-definition that you're creating in your own mind. Aware of your ears listening. Aware of me speaking. Aware of the traffic outside. Aware of the feelings in your body. Aware of your mind grabbing at this and that. Just sit with me in this awareness. There is nothing we have to do; just come into this moment. Don't collect it; don't judge it. Just bring in more awareness. Watch your mind. Listen to yourself. Feel your heart. Is it flowing? Breathe in and out of the middle of your chest, as if there were a flow moving in and out of your heart with every breath. Flowing. Present. Here. More here. More. Let go of your expectations a little more. Of your definitions of who you are, of what God is. Of where you're going, of where you've come from. Of your emotions: sadness, happiness. Don't push them away. Notice them. Acknowledge them. Give them space. They are all part of the flow. Your senses, your memories, your plans, your models; all of it. Passing show. Forms being created, existing, and disappearing back into formlessness. Here in the moment. Right here. For the end result of everything that you and I have been sharing for years and years is not there or then or "maybe" or "perhaps" or "if only" or "as soon as I. . . ." This is it.

Look at the stuff in you that's keeping you from being here at this moment. Judging. Waiting. Trying to experience. *I can't get it. I still feel separate.* That thought—there's the problem right there.

Let it go. The quiet mind. Choiceless awareness. Perfect flow and harmony. No you. No self-consciousness. Not, "I am trying to become enlightened." In meditation, there is no meditator. Meditation just *is*. Meditation is the act of openness. Of spaciousness. Of presence. Of is-ness.

So why are we joining all these clubs? Why are we paying all these heavy dues? What is it all about? Are all methods to be avoided? It doesn't seem so. But it does seem useful to see them in perspective. Methods are the ship crossing the ocean of existence. If we're halfway across the ocean, it's a little silly to decide methods are unnecessary if we don't know how to swim. But once we get to the far shore, it would be useless to keep carrying the boat. The game seems very simple: methods are not the thing itself; methods are traps. We entrap ourselves in order to burn out things in us that keep us from being free. And ultimately the methods spew us out at the other end, and the method disintegrates into nothingness. Every method: the Guru, chanting, study, meditation, practices, all of it. For the end result is "nothing special."

If we take knowing God as being always in meditation as we act all day long; as choiceless awareness; as being clear with no attachments, judgments, or opinions, no clinging, no pushing and pulling, no this or that—we will experience what it means to know and be in God.

But if there are any experiences that we crave other than being free of the separation between experiencer and experience, that's what we need to concern ourselves with—not with fear about our cravings, but bringing to them consciousness and truth and quietness. For every teacher, every life experience, everything we notice in the universe is a reflection of our attachments. That's just the way it works. If there is nothing we want, there is nothing that clings. We go through life free, collecting nothing. When we collect a sight, or collect a picture, or a record, or a relationship, or a teacher, or methods, it's just more clinging. Use them all, be with them, enjoy them, live fully in life; but don't cling. Flow through it, be with it, let it go. As we quiet and listen to hear how it all is, then we will relate to all of it in a harmonious way, in a way in which there is no exploitation, harmonious in the way we relate to the floor we're sitting on, to the person next to us, to the night air, to the world we have to live in.

If I can hear it, right where I am, whatever space I might be in at that moment, when there is no clinging, when I am neither attached to emptiness nor form, I am free. If I push away the physical existence in order to get into "a space," if I'm only comfortable when I'm hanging out with Krishna and I can't stand my mother-in-law, I'm trapped. No clinging anywhere. And then the moment gets so rich, it's all right here. Every astral plane, physical plane, every level of consciousness, every mental state, all the emptiness: all of it, right here. Only a quiet mind hears it all.

It's our purity that calls forth the teachings; it's our acknowledgment of who we are. It's our quietness; it's just opening ourselves to the space we exist in. Instead of judging and pushing and pulling, opening to it, just consuming the stuff, letting it all flow through us and in and out of us—just allowing it to pass.

If our method is Vipassana meditation, we're just noticing everything in the universe around us with bare attention. Maybe starting with the simple thing of noticing the breath go in and out of our nostrils, or go up and down in the solar plexus. The things we'll have to let go of are self-pity, feelings of unworthiness, feelings of inadequacy, clinging to a judging mind, attachments to desires that see things as objects, which push the universe away. There is simply awareness noticing each element of the mind-body process as it comes and goes, but "nobody" watching.

If our method is the Guru, then we look at the Guru, and the Guru keeps changing before our eyes. First we've got this form, and then this form falls away, and then that form falls away. It's like Chinese puzzle boxes. We keep opening them, and there's more inside. And we keep going until we realize we're just looking at a mirror. And all we're doing is cleaning; we're peeling ourselves like an onion. And as we get purer, we see more of our Guru until, finally, it's just one mirror looking at another, and no dust anywhere. Then there's no mirror. There's nothing. Our Guru disappeared into our own enlightenment. We and the Guru became one in God. That's the way the game works. That's the method of the Guru.

We should be open to all teachers and all teachings, and listen with our hearts. With some we will feel we have no business. Others will pull us. We must trust ourselves. We have everything in us that Buddha has, that Christ has—we've got it all. But only when we start to acknowledge it will it get interesting. Our problem is we're afraid to acknowledge our own beauty. We're too busy holding on to our unworthiness. We'd rather be a schnook sitting before some great man. That fits in more with who we think we are. Well, enough already. We are beautiful.

Do you realize, historically, how rare it is that this kind of a dialogue has existed, with this much consciousness in it?

Once we find our lineage—and we can't go looking for it, we

will be drawn to it, and it may not be in the form of a single teacher—it may simply be a way in which we view the universe. And through surrender into this lineage, every act we do will be done from a space of greater clarity, will be an act determined not by our personal desires but by the dharmic moment. It will be pulled forth from us, just as these words are pulled forth from me by you. I have no identification with them. This book is just the transcript of words spoken to us listening, demanding that they be spoken. So whose book is it? When beautiful music is played on a violin, would you go up and thank the violin? I'm just the mouthpiece for a process. What we're doing through this book is touching ourselves. Forget me; I am passing show. We're touching ourselves. Sooner or later we're going to have to acknowledge our beauty. But that acknowledgment isn't the end point. That's merely to override the acknowledgment of our ugliness, to which we've been clinging. Then both of them are going to have to go, for the end point isn't self-consciousness, sitting around like Narcissus saying, "Look how beautiful I am." The end point is just being in the present moment.

When we finish with our lineage and we get spewed out the other end, then we'll look around, and we'll see that all methods get to the top of the mountain. And that we can find God in everyone. Then we no longer are Buddhists or Hindus or Christians or Jews or Muslims. We are love. We are truth. And love and truth have no form. They flow into forms. But the word is never the same as that which the word connotes. The word *God* is not God, the word *Mother* is not Mother, the word *Self* is not Self, the word *moment* is not the moment. All of these words are empty. We're playing at the level of intellect, feeding that thing in us that keeps wanting to understand. And here we are—all the words we've said are gone. Where did they go? Do you remember them all? Empty, empty. If we heard them, we are at this moment empty. We're ready for the next word. And the word will go through us. We don't have to know anything; that's what's so funny about it. We get so simple. We're empty. We know nothing. We simply are wisdom. Not becoming anything, just being everything.

Chapter 14

God and Beyond

All the time I was with Maharaj-ji, he never had me meditate. He'd feed me, love me, pat me, yell at me, cajole me, bore me, fascinate me, perplex me, send me away, draw me to him. Yet, when I told him I was going to do a Buddhist meditation retreat, he said to me, "Bring your mind to one-pointedness, and you will know God." When somebody showed him a book in which there was a picture of Kalu Rinpoche on one side and him on the other, he pointed to one picture and said, "Buddha," and then pointed to the other and said, "Buddha."

One morning when I was in Allahabad at a house where Maharaj-ji was staying, maybe fifteen or twenty Indian devotees came to see him. About thirty Westerners sat around the outside of the circle. One of the Indians who came in was obviously a very important man. I never could get clear whether he was a Supreme Court judge or an administrative director of the court. When he came in, I was very content being in the back with all of the Westerners and watching the whole process.

Suddenly Maharaj-ji started to build up my image to this

man, saying, "This is Dr. Alpert from America. He is a professor at Harvard . . . a great saint."

And the Supreme Court judge turned and said, "Well, perhaps you'd like to visit the court."

Now, I come from a family of lawyers, and I've spent more than enough time in courts. I was in India to be with Maharaj-ji and didn't want to visit the court, but I was caught in my social propriety, so I said, "Well, that would be lovely."

And then he said, "Well, tomorrow at ten?"

And I felt I was being trapped from the abstract to the concrete, so I said, "Well, you'll have to ask my Guru," figuring that he would get me off the hook.

But Maharaj-ji said, "If Ram Dass said it'd be lovely, it'll be lovely. He'll go at ten." And then he pointed at me like, *Watch it, baby; you lie, you'll pay. Captain Karma will get you.* So I went to the court and watched a murder trial and then went to the law library, and the librarian was a great student of the *Ramayana;* we talked about Ram and Hanuman, then we went into the bar review room where all the lawyers hang out. And all the lawyers saw me, a Westerner, being escorted by this very important man whom they were all being very obsequious to. So they came over and tried to discuss Nixon's China policy with me. At that moment it was of great concern to India, and I had just read *Time Magazine,* so I was in a perfect position to be an expert. So I discussed power blocks, Russia, and alignments; I did a perfect snow job.

When I came back, Maharaj-ji kept asking me, "Well, what happened at the court?" And every time I'd go to tell him, he'd tell me because he obviously had watched the whole process from some other level, so I thought it was over and I had learned my lesson. Well, that evening the head of the law association came to have darshan with Maharaj-ji. And he said to me, "We were thinking that you might perhaps address the Rotary Club and the Honorary Legal Society."

I thought, *Oh no, I'm going to end up on the creamed vegetable circuit.* So I said, "I really don't want to. You'll have to ask Maharaj-ji." I didn't even get into being nice. I thought I'd be really truthful. *But,* I thought, *if Maharaj-ji tells me I've got to do it, I'll do it.*

So he goes up and says, "Maharaj-ji, we would love to have Dr. Alpert address the Honorary Legal Society and the Rotary Club."

Maharaj-ji looked delighted. When you knew Maharaj-ji, who sat with a blanket and a watering pot and couldn't care less, you knew it was all nonsense from where he was sitting. But, oh, he was fascinated. And he was saying to everybody, "Ram Dass is going to speak at the Rotary Club," as if to say, "This is it! We've finally broken through. We're going big time now."

And my heart was sinking. For half a moment, I thought, *He just was hustling me. He wants to exploit me to become big time in India. Oh damn it, I've been had again.*

And then he said to me, "Well what are you going to talk about?" He was terribly interested.

And I said, "Well, I don't know, Maharaj-ji. I guess I'll talk about Law as Dharma." I was grasping at something quick to be cute about.

And he says, "Uh-huh, are you going to talk about Hanuman?"

And I said, "Oh, of course, Maharaj-ji."

He said, "That's good."

And I saw the lawyer's face take on a peculiar change.

And then Maharaj-ji said, "Are you going to talk about me?"

"Of course, Maharaj-ji," I said. "You're my Guru."

"Well, that's good. Are you going to talk about Christ?"

"Absolutely."

So the lawyer said, "Well, we kind of thought he'd talk about Nixon's China policy."

And Maharaj-ji turned to him and said, "Oh no, Ram Dass is not to be trusted about worldly things. He can only talk about God; that's all he's capable of talking about. Ram Dass only talks about God."

I said, "That's right. I only talk about God."

And the lawyer said, "Well, in that case, perhaps he shouldn't speak to the group. Maybe I'll have a few lawyers who are interested come by my house." Suddenly the whole thing lost its interest to a very worldly group of people.

And I thought, *Perfect! I've just been given my instructions. All I've got to do is talk about God for the rest of my life, and I'm protected. I don't have to get lost in all the worldly stuff.* But I came back to the West, and it's funny to talk about God in the West. It's not easy to talk about. It's not that God is dead; it's just that God is not a viable concept.

I still talk about God a lot, but it's tricky, because I am more than superficially trained in Buddhism. And Buddhist philosophy does not really involve itself with the concept of God. I am very attracted to the simplicity and cleanness of Theravada and Zen Buddhism. So on the one hand, I'm faced with the Zen part of myself, which finds the concept of God an unnecessary addition to a simple universe. And on the other, I have my Guru, who says, "Speak only about God."

Now the world, the universe, looks different as our consciousness shifts. Most of us start as psychological beings identified with our psychological accumulations. We are emotional, thinking, feeling entities. In Buddhism we learn about anicca, dukkha, anatta—the changeability, unsatisfactoriness, and emptiness of all phenomena. We learn about the impermanence of things, of thoughts, the passing nature of all states of being, feelings, concepts. We learn about the suffering that is caused by clinging to these concepts. And finally, with anatta, we find that even the concept of self must go—whether that self is physical self, or psychological self, or astral self, or soul self, or the Eternal Self. Concepts are concepts; and concepts must go. And even the concept of enlightenment or Nirvana or that which is beyond self is just another concept. So why would we as psychological beings who are here with all of our problems and melodramas and attempts and strivings and awakenings and all that—why would we want to buy into more concepts when the game is to get rid of them and go beyond concepts? God is a concept. Soul is a concept. And when I say I am a spiritual entity who has taken birth in order to work out my karma, there is no "me" in truth whose karma must be worked out. There is only an apparent grouping of events, one of which is the concept we have of ourselves. And it all dissolves through deeper and deeper meditation, and more and more emptying. We disappear along with the universe into the Void.

Well, what I have come to understand is that my path involves my heart, involves flow. It can't come after the fact. It has to be the leading edge of my method. And in a devotional path, we work with forms in order to transform our own identities. And, in the process, we break the habits we've held as our realities and

our own self-definitions. And the new realities, the new concepts
we take on, because they were taken on intentionally, don't have
the same hold over us that the old ones had. It's using a skillful
means to get rid of one thing when later we will get rid of that aid
as well. Ramana Maharshi refers to these concepts, specifically
the concept of "I" or "Self," as the stick that you use to stir the
funeral pyre. If you go to Benares, you'll find the bodies being
burned at the burning ghat while men with big sticks stir the
embers to make sure the whole thing gets burned. And after they
finish stirring a particular fire, as it's getting near the end, they
throw the stick on the fire and it too burns up.

And so it is with Gurus, teachers, methods, and God—for what
God is, is beyond the concept of God. It's exactly the same thing
as the Gate Gate Paragate Parasamgate Bodhi Svaha mantra.
It's beyond the concept of beyond. Now in Judaism, except in the
Hasid tradition a bit, the closest you get to God is coming into His
presence, but dualism remains right to the end. It's ultimately still
dualistic, I and Thou. It is blasphemy within traditional Judaism
to conceive of merging with God; for God is unknowable—it's G-d,
it's unspeakable. It's the word that can't be spoken.

From my point of view as a heart being, as a devotional being,
I have a Guru, and there is Hanuman, there is Durga, there is
Krishna, there is Ram, there is Jesus, there is Buddha, there is
Ramakrishna, there is Ramana Maharshi. My universe is peopled
with these beings. They are no less real than we are. The only difference between them and us is that they know they are not real
and are free. We are still thinking, attached to what we think we
think. And they aren't. They are what's called the sangha in Buddhism, or satsang in Hinduism, the community of beings that

I hang out with. There is nothing that comes out of them that is going to entrap me because they know it's all lila, all just the cosmic dance of being.

I sat before Maharaj-ji—before this man in a blanket—just loving him. All I wanted to do was caress his foot. It's extraordinary to love somebody that much. I was in ecstasy just looking at him. I'd been doing that for months and months, and finally I thought, *Maybe this is just the veil; I've got to go beyond the veil.* One day I was sitting across the courtyard from him, and everybody was up around him, and I thought, *I don't have to be around him. This is just form. Look—they're all worshipping the form. The form isn't it. I don't have to be here.* Just then Maharaj-ji turned and looked at me, and then sent an old man over to touch my feet. I asked him why he did it, and he replied, "Maharaj-ji said, 'Go over and touch Ram Dass's feet because he and I understand each other perfectly.'" Because at that moment I was seeing through the method that I was using. I wasn't stopping my love for him, but I wasn't trapped by it anymore.

Now, I could talk about the Dharmic Law, but it's very hard for many people to fall in love with a Dharmic Law. But it's very easy for me to fall in love with God. But the concept of God is very much the same as the concept of the Dharmic Law. It's the law of the relationship of things. It's the original consciousness; it's the one mind; it's the Ancient One. It's that which at its heart is empty. I'd sit before Maharaj-ji and think, *I'm not going to be taken by the form.* So while he'd be handing out stuff, I'd be meditating with my eyes closed, focusing on my third eye, and I would start to feel this change coming over my body, and I'd feel more and more energy. And suddenly, with my eyes closed,

I would meet him on a different astral plane. Now, you can get fascinated with that. That's the whole world of the occult; all those forces and beings to play with. "But Maharaj-ji, that isn't who you are either." And I'd go right through that one too. It's like going through infinite doorways. You come to another one, and you think that door is the final temple, and then you see it's just another doorway, and you go through it. And you go through another, and another. And if you go through far enough, you come right back to yourself, which isn't either. The whole thing, method and all, just disintegrates before your eyes.

When I sit with Maharaj-ji, my heart flows. I flow into the universe of forms, and the universe of forms flows into me. As that flow gets greater and greater, the boundaries between Maharaj-ji and me disappear. For me, Maharaj-ji is the universe, so that the differentiation between me and the universe disappears into a flow of energy. As I open more and more through my heart, and thus become more and more of the flow of the universe in its energy form, I start to rise. It's as if it's a fuel. And I rise into states of consciousness that are known as jhanic states or samadhi states. Each experience is another form of Maharaj-ji, or the Mother—and must be consumed, for Maharaj-ji must be consumed by me, taken into myself; I must surrender into him until there is no boundary. He is not only all the forms that are available to my physical eye but also those I perceive with my spiritual eye. And as I go into higher and higher states, there are fewer and fewer forms. And many of the forms are only half-formed, for they are on the edge of where the form and formless meet.

On the way through these planes are experiences of emptiness and coldness and impersonality. They are not empty because they are "experiences" of emptiness. That's different. There are planes or states of incredible bliss and rapture, where your whole body is writhing in delight. It's as though every cell were having an orgasm. There are states or planes of consciousness of diamond clarity, in which you see and know and understand everything's relationship to everything else. It's as if you are privy to the secrets of God. There are planes or states of consciousness where everything is aesthetically so perfect, even the words come out as poetry, and all is luminous and colorful. Aldous Huxley writes about that. Aldous once said, "The reason we like precious jewels so much is they remind us of planes of consciousness we've lived on where those are the pebbles." Form after form, plane after plane, state after state, experience after experience—all within Maharaj-ji, all within my love and my flow toward other. And there comes a point where the flow is so open and the boundaries are so far erased that you and Maharaj-ji, or you and the Mother, or you and the form, become one, at every level of form, all the way up to pure, undifferentiated energy.

Were that the end, it would be so easy for our minds to grasp, so easy for science to control. But all of that is just a doorway. All of that merely brings us to the edge of the lake. It is at the edge of the lake that we experience the presence of what lies beyond form. Yet there is no "what" that lies beyond form, for there is no beyond, for what *it* is contains all that is. We, at that moment, sit at the edge where we *are* the paradox. All of the forms disappear into the lake of emptiness, and yet they are not lost. It's at the edge of the lake that someone whose path is the path of the heart will say, "I am experiencing the presence of God," for one more step into the lake and the experiencer and the experience have merged, and we have become God, and the concept of God is long gone. As we merge into God, we have entered into what the Buddhists call Nirvana. The game is not to know God; the game is to be God. To be God is to be nobody, and yet there is nothing that we are not.

If we come back into form from having merged with God, we are in the world, though not of it. We play the cosmic sport. We fill the forms, though there is no one home; it is just more lila, the dance of God.

There are beings who have roamed, and do roam, this earth and other planes of consciousness, who have entered into that ocean and returned. Their existence liberates all who recognize them. We may have in our midst such a being, but we would never know it, because we are attached to the form. We might be like someone catching an apple from Maharaj-ji and failing to recognize that there is nobody throwing the apple. So while he is God beckoning from beyond, we get lost along the path. And because God does not exist in time, he doesn't push us—for, sooner or later, one lifetime or another, we get home. And when we get home, we will realize that we have always been God—that we created our own separateness for the sport. The difference between us and a Guru or a perfected being is that they aren't, and we still think we are.

Christ said, "I have come to bring you to the Father. I am in the Father; the Father is in me. You know not who I am. Let those that have ears, hear." Quiet the mind; be free of clinging to molds and models and thought forms. Open the heart. Consume the emotions into the flow, the flow of all forms of life, until you are just flowing in and out.

As we get more disciplined, we keep the energy moving toward that point where form and formless meet. Were we to stay in the formless, our bodies—which we left behind—would disintegrate, for there would be no consciousness to keep them going. There are all gradations, and some beings are 99 percent in that ocean of formlessness and leave behind just a thread in form. There was a being walled up in a cave for twenty years; every year devotees would go to see him and have darshan with what was a skeleton, except the hair and the nails kept growing. He just left a thread behind to give darshan to the devotees.

Krishna, Christ, Hanuman—all of them the same. The ocean made manifest in different forms. Different strokes for different folks. Each a form we need, if we need form.

Chapter 15

Questions and Answers

I really want to be a good yogi, and I am trying very hard to purify myself, but it's so hard. What's wrong?

Purification is an act of letting go. In one of the Gospels it says that men need not disfigure their faces in order to know God. There is a type of righteousness and seriousness that creeps in the minute we decide we're going to do spiritual practices. Suddenly it's serious work, and we have to be a certain kind of way—sort of tight-assed. We may find that, though it looks good from the outside, it begins to feel kind of lousy from the inside. And there is a way in which denying too much stops the flow of spiritual energy. There are a lot of people who are really good meditators, who sit perfectly and their minds get very quiet. But they aren't liberated—because they have pushed away form, they've pushed away the earth, they've pushed away the heart, they've pushed away flow.

If I understand this game at all, it's a game of exquisite balancing. And the balancing can be understood within different systems. For example, in southern Buddhist meditation, Theravada Buddhist meditation, three components are emphasized. One is called sila, one is called samadhi, and one is called panna. Sila is the purification: nonkilling, nonstealing, nonlying, right speech, right livelihood, and so on. Samadhi is concentration and mindfulness. And panna is right understanding and right thought, or the wisdom connected with it.

Now, if we watch the way the game works with those three components—purification, concentration, and wisdom—we'll see that we wouldn't even start this dance without a little bit of wisdom. We have to understand a little bit of what the game is about even to want to sit and meditate. So we have a little bit of panna, and then we try to do samadhi, concentration. But every time we try to concentrate, all of our other desires, all of our other connections and clingings to the world keep pulling on us all the time. So we have to clean up our game a little bit; that's called sila, purification. We clean up our game a little bit, and then our meditation gets a little deeper. As our meditation gets a little deeper, we are quieter and we are able to see more of the universe so that wisdom gets deeper and we understand more. The deeper panna makes it easier to let go of some of the attachments, so it makes it easier to increase the sila. And the increased sila allows the samadhi to get deeper. So we begin to see the way these three things all keep interweaving with one another. They're a beautiful balancing act.

Now, in the same way, in other lineages, there are balancings that can be understood in other ways. One way is to talk about the heart and the mind—that is, flow and quietness. Another balance is to talk about form and formless. Another way of saying that is to talk about the Mother and the Father. Still another way of talking about a balance is talking about shakti and love or power and flow. Some people get symptoms of shakti—pressure in the head, shaking, movements, twitching, nausea, pains in the back, all kinds of symptoms—because of the lack of the balance, because they're too much into the shakti realm without the flow. But we begin to be able to diagnose our own predicament in our own bodies, in our own beings, to ascertain what is out of balance and to come back into the flow. Because getting the powers, the yogic powers, the siddhis, without the love, without the flow, without the compassion, makes you just another power tripper. Our society is full of people who have siddhis, who have powers. They have power of the intellect, and they have power of the mind to control others. But the compassion isn't there. The heart isn't open.

On the other hand, people who have heart, lots of love but no control, no discipline, no one-pointedness tend to get very mushy. They're like soft earth—there's nothing firm in them, and that lack of firmness keeps allowing them to go only so far, and they keep falling down again. There's no backbone in the process.

The way to approach the whole sadhana is with firmness and with lightness. Not hysterical *ha*, *ha*, *ha* but with a lightness, a delight, enjoying the light of it all, making it light. Somewhere I remember a line that goes, "The angels can fly 'cause they take themselves lightly." People tend to get very lost in their own melodramas, romanticizing their own spiritual journey. "I'm getting enlightened." And they tend to take themselves very seriously. They've got themselves a storyline. And they begin to look like yogis, and they begin to smell like yogis, and they come on as they imagine yogis should; they have a whole image of themselves becoming yogis. That's all going to have to go. We come back into the present moment. We are what we are. We let go of the romantic storyline of our own predicament, because that one's just keeping us from being wherever we really are at the moment.

I'd just like to point out that righteousness, being very "good," does not necessarily bring us to truth. Once we are wedded to and immersed in truth, in the sense of formlessness, then we will be righteous. It's like the Ten Commandments. We can do them out of a "goody-goody" place, with anger in our hearts, and righteousness and fear of punishment; or we can come into the space of our own being in relation to God, where we look and see why things are the way they are; and it just flows out of us and we just can't act in ways that create more karma or lay trips on other human beings. Then we begin to understand the Ten Commandments from a different angle—righteousness coming out of truth, rather than truth coming out of righteousness.

My son has developed a neurotic habit that worries me and my wife quite a bit. What should we do?

To the extent that you are free of the attachment to how it ought to be with your son and with your identity as a father, with being able to be a father perfectly—I'm not talking about abrogating responsibility for safety and survival, just about not getting lost in fatherness—you can see him as a being who is living out a certain incarnation in which this neurotic pattern is showing. By contacting that being behind the neurotic pattern, you can help him drop it when he's ready to drop it.

My understanding of the way a child grows is that you create the garden, you don't grow the flower. You can merely fertilize the earth and keep it soft and moist, and then the flower grows as best it can. You create a space with your consciousness that determines whether the neurotic pattern gets deeper into that child or whether it's seen as something that can be cast off when the time comes. If you define this being as "my child who has this habit," and that's the major reality of the relationship between you and the child, that's catching him in the habit. The minute you see him as a soul who's incarnated in this situation in which he's working through this stuff, he's free to drop it whenever he needs to, because you're not attached to his having it or not having it.

It's an interesting one, because people get guilty that they're not doing enough about their children, and they tend to get caught in this sort of predicament. You don't change your wife or your child. You just keep working on yourself until you are such a clear mirror reflection, such a supportive rock of love for all those beings that everybody is free to give up their stuff when they want to give it up—your wife, her anxiety; your child, that habit. You keep creating a space in which people can grow when they're ready to grow.

The predicament is that a child and a parent may be at very different levels of evolution in terms of their ages of being. A child could be much older than the parent, or much younger than the parent, in an evolutionary sense. There are many old beings being born into this culture at this moment. They have been looking to take birth in a conscious environment, so that some of you have babies that don't particularly want to be incarnated because they're almost beyond it. They're just doing some little clean-up operation.

The minute we do a "take" of beings as souls rather than personalities and bodies, we don't cling to the incarnation that hard. We understand its function, and we don't demand that the incarnation be other than it is. We understand that births are consciously chosen to work out specific karmic necessities, and we don't get as lost in the melodrama on this plane.

It's very tricky which level of reality you climb into. The power of conscious beings is that they don't use one against the other. They keep all those levels of consciousness going simultaneously. So if somebody is brought in on a stretcher to see me, and she's in terrible pain, and she has been for years, and at one level I can see that she's doing a tremendous amount of work in this life, and at another, *God, this person is suffering so badly. Can I do anything to relieve the suffering?* Both of those thoughts occur at the same moment consciously. And if that person who is brought to me is somebody who says, "I wish to awaken during this lifetime; Ram Dass, help me," then I say to her, "Well, you're really feeling sorry for yourself. You've really got a good birth; you're cleaning up a lot of stuff. Let's work on how to convert pain." And if she is somebody who didn't say that, but we just happen to meet, like somebody's aunt or something like that, I say, "God, it's really rough how much you're suffering. Here, let me fix the pillow for you," or "Are you having proper medical treatment?" or "What can I do for you?"

It's very interesting how you deal with problems and suffering depending upon which plane of consciousness is the dominant theme, although you never forget the other one. A strong consciousness keeps it all going at the same time. You do everything you can to help your son feel more loved, calm, supported, and ready to get rid of the neurotic habits—and at the same moment, you are not attached and you understand that it is the karma of this being that is being lived out, and you work on yourself until you are a perfect environment for that being to do what it needs to do.

How do you interpret dreams?

In general, I'm inclined to suggest we shouldn't do too much analytic work in this dance, because our minds play too many tricks. If the dream has an immediate significance that affects you emotionally, work with it. It may help click into place something you needed to understand about yourself. Fine. But if you say, "I wonder what that meant," forget it! It fits under the category of things that when you're ready to know, you'll know. Don't sit and analyze or wonder or get preoccupied with it. It all has meaning. It's all work you're doing on other planes. It is significant spiritually, but you don't always have to understand it.

You exist on many planes simultaneously at this moment. The only reason you don't know of your other identities is because you're so attached to this one. But this one or that one—don't get lost; don't stick anywhere; it's all just more stuff. Go for broke, awake totally.

You say every life situation is a perfect lesson. How is that so?

The universe is made up of experiences that are designed to burn out our reactivity, which is our attachment, our clinging, to pain, to pleasure, to fear, to all of it. And as long as there are places where we're vulnerable, the universe will find ways to confront us with them. That's the way the dance is designed. In truth, there are millions and millions of stimuli that we are not even noticing, that go by, in every plane of existence, all the time. The reason we don't notice or react to them is because we have no attachment to them. They don't stir our desire system. Our desires affect our perception.

Each of us is living in our own universe, created out of our projected attachments. That's what we mean when we say, "You create your own universe." We are creating that universe because of our attachments, which can also be avoidances and fears. As we develop spiritually and see how it all is, more and more we keep consuming and neutralizing our own reactivity. Each time we see ourselves reacting we're saying, "Right, and this situation too, and this one too, Tat Tvam Asi, and that also, and that also, and that also." Gradually the attachments start to lose their pull and to fall away.

We get so that we're perfectly willing to do whatever we do— and to do it perfectly and without attachment. It's like Mahatma Gandhi gets put in jail and they give him a lice-infested uniform and tell him to clean the latrines, and it's a whole mess. And he walks up to the head of the guards and he says, in total truth, "Thank you." He's not putting them on or up-leveling them. He's saying, "There's a teaching here, and I'm getting it; thank you." What's bizarre is that we get to the point where somebody lays a heavy trip on us and we get caught, and then we see through our *caughtness* and we say, "Thank you." We may not say it aloud because it's too cute. But we feel, *Thank you.* People come up and are violent or angry or write nasty letters or whatever they do to express their frustration or anger or competition, and all I can say is thanks.

When an oppressor, or an oppressive economic system, is causing people suffering, it seems to me not enough to love the individual who is oppressing along with those who are being oppressed. It seems that if one were to really love them, one would speak out. I fear that many of us who seek, feel that it is no longer necessary to criticize in such a manner.

You are raising the question about our social responsibility for political inequities, social inequities. Where is our responsibility? Is it enough to meditate? Is it enough to become a loving person?

Well, our predicament is this: We are in an incarnation. We can't make believe we're not. We must honor the attendant responsibilities that go along with that incarnation—parents, political identities, social identities, and work—in form, in order to alleviate the suffering at whatever level we find it. Now, the peculiar predicament is that when we see any kind of injustice in the world, if we are attached to anger about it, or are attached to it being any other way, we are at one level perpetuating the polarization even as we are working to end it.

In Patanjali's *Ashtanga Yoga*, it says there is no giving and no receiving. Does that mean that nobody gives and nobody receives? No. It means that when we give, we are not attached to being the giver. Thus, we do not force the other person to be the receiver. Their political inequities are our political inequities. There is no "them" in the universe. There is only "us," more or less pure. And we, as a collectivity, must purify ourselves. Each individual must hear her or his dharma—that is, the way in which the manifestation must come forth in order to relieve suffering. Until we are enlightened, all action is an exercise in working on our own consciousness. The forms, however, will differ. For example, if somebody comes up to me as my friend Wavy Gravy did once and tells me that it only costs ten cents a day to keep a starving person alive in a third-world country, his coming along and telling me that creates a new situation in which I now exist. That situation elicits from me a set of behaviors to do what I can do—so I do a benefit to raise money to help and have that money go to help feed starving children. If Wavy had not said that to me, I probably would not have done that.

We can't walk away from life on this plane. For instance, I feel it is dharmic for me to be involved in politics to the extent that I vote, make my opinions known to my congressional representatives, and sometimes join political actions.

There are a thousand and one ways in which humans are unjust to fellow humans. Which ones will we work to change? Which are our particular dharmic paths? As we work to alleviate suffering, will we be careful that the way in which we do it doesn't create more suffering in the long run? Be conscious. Since we're not fully enlightened, everything we do must be done as work on ourselves. At the same moment, we must listen to hear what form our efforts must take to relieve suffering.

You may run a nursery, you may just help an elderly lady across the street, you may go into the Peace Corps, you may join a community service, you may go to Washington and work actively in politics, you may work in a free health clinic, you may become a concert guitarist, or you may raise your children with great love and consciousness. We are not in the position of judging each other. Each person must hear his own dharmic way. What you feel is most important may not be seen as most important to someone else. This is a very complex society we are a part of. Stay in the world, do your part, raise your children, earn your living, and assume your responsibility at every level. Do it all as an exercise to bring you to God, because until you are one with God, every act you perform will both liberate and entrap. And if you are really interested in ending suffering, you recognize that the end of suffering is full awareness. And only an aware person can help another person become aware.

It's only because we forgot the First Commandment in the first place that we're dealing with all this right now. So now we're in the process of remembering. It's very simple.

What's the best way to deal with the judging mind?

Watch it. Watch it do its thing. There it is judging again. Very simple. If we're working with Christ, we can offer it up to Christ. If we're working with Vipassana meditation, we would merely take the primary object of meditation, which might be following the breath, and then every time a judgmental thought came up, we'd note, "Judgmental thought," or something like that, and then we'd go right back to the breath. It's just another thought.

Thoughts keep clothing themselves in all kinds of silk and glitter, and they say, "I'm not just another thought . . . I'm *you*." You know. "I'm real. This judgment is the *real* thought." But it's just another thought. This whole game is just thought.

After a really good meditation, I feel like I'm not in my body.

You very well may not be; it's true. I must admit that I am of the school of hard knocks. I'm not going to protect us from confronting all of our attachments. The reason we may not be in our bodies after meditation is because we don't *want* to come back into our bodies. We're attached to the high. Okay. Confront it. If we're aware of it enough to complain about it, we're seeing our own predicament. I think that we are not brought through by a spoon-fed operation. Maharaj-ji would allow me to enter absorption states in which my body would be shaking and the breath would become all but nonexistent; then he'd say to the interpreter, "Ask Ram Dass how much money Steven makes." I'd struggle to ignore him, but he'd demand I come back immediately. We learn after a while that we have control, that we can do all this stuff. There's no real need to protect us from ourselves. We're just seeing our own attachments.

Why did it all begin? Why did we leave God in the first place?

That is the question which is the ultimate question, and Buddha's answer to that question was, "It's none of our business." Which is not a facetious answer. He's saying our subject-object mind can't know the answer to that question. It's an answer that we can be, but we can't know; because in order to know that, we would have to be that from which it started, but we aren't it as long as we're asking the question.

It's one of those kinds of absurdities that we get caught in. There are a dozen different answers, all of which are equally real and unreal. We might say God took form in order to know himself, that he had to become separate in order to see himself. Or it could be said that since there is no time at another level of reality, nothing happened anyway. That's a real answer too. These are all valid answers within one level of reality or another. Every level has its own answer to that question, but the answer is not truly knowable until we have transcended those levels, because any answer we give is just feeding our minds from one level or another, and they're all only relatively true.

Now, that all sounds like words, which means it's not an appropriate question. We keep asking it, but we won't get an answer. I mean, not only from me; the answer is not in words.

What is shakti, or prana?

Shakti, or prana, is the universal stuff from which it all comes. Everything here is shakti; it's all just shakti, patterns of shakti. It's the stuff of the universe, finer than quanta of energy in the physical, scientific realm. We can ignore it if our method does not involve focusing on energy, or we can work with it, draw it in, mobilize it, direct it, and use it as a force. We can use it in the same way we might use electricity—we can collect it in the same way. It feels the same, except it is much finer. We can draw it in and draw it in and draw it in, and we will experience new realms of perception and new powers.

Before we are done, we will be subject to, or must surrender to, intensities of energy that grow and grow and grow, until they are nothing short of all of the energy of the universe, and to the extent that there are impurities within us, or paranoia, or a body that is not kept in a good shape, when we start to tune in on these higher energies, we can really blow our circuits, or shake ourselves very badly. When we see people shaking, all that bouncing energy stuff, that doesn't have to be. That is because the person is trying to put 220 volts into a 110-volt system. The process of purification is preparing ourselves as containers to handle more and more energy, more and more love—and for that we need quieter and quieter minds, and stronger bodies, and more open hearts.

There are a lot of different traditions, some of which are very much oriented around shakti—Kundalini Yoga, for instance. Others recognize and use these energies in another manner. When we just work with shakti, we get great power. But unless that shakti is perfectly balanced with wisdom, and the empty mind, and love, it can be extremely destructive. Similarly, if we only work with our intellect and with the emptying of our mind, as in some yogas, and we fail to open our heart, our journey becomes very dry and brittle. Ultimately, no matter what our methods, we have to get a very even balance between our energy, heart, and mind.

How does LSD affect the spiritual journey?

My first struggle with that was in a correspondence with Meher Baba back in 1965, in which he said that very few people can use it positively; for many people it will make them insane. And I wrote, *It's strange, Meher Baba, but the only reason I read your books is because I took acid, and that's true of many devotees that follow you in America.* And he wrote back and said, *I know you're a good person, and for a few people it can be helpful; but for most it's not helpful; and you can take it three more times.*

Well, I didn't listen to Meher Baba; I took it a number of times more than that. Then in 1967 or '68, Maharaj-ji asked me about that "medicine" that I used in the West, and he took 900 micrograms, as you may know from *Be Here Now*. Nothing happened at all to him, which was impressive. I must admit, though, that because nothing happened, I went through a little doubt. I thought maybe he threw them over his shoulder, maybe they never got in his mouth. It all happened so fast, and when you're around somebody like that, you're so stoned, who knows? So I had this little doubt, but I came back and told everybody he took 900 micrograms.

In 1970, when I was in India the next time, he said, "Ram Dass, did you give me some medicine the last time you were in India?"

"Yes," I said.

"Did I take it?" he asked, with a little twinkle in his eye.

I said, "Well, I think so."

He said, "What happened?"

And I said, "Nothing, Maharaj-ji."

And he said, "Jao! Jao! Go away."

The next morning he said, "Do you have any more medicine?"

So I brought out what I had left, and he took 1,200 micrograms this time. He took each tablet and stuck it in his mouth and made sure that I saw, and he munched them up. Then he said, "Can I have water?"

I said, "Yes."

And he asked, "Will the medicine make me insane?"

So I said, "Probably."

So he said, "How long will it take?"

I said, "An hour at the most."

So he got an old man up there with a watch, and he was holding it and looking at it. And he drank a lot of water. And about halfway through, he started to look really weird; he even went under his blanket, and he came up looking totally insane. *Oh my God,* I thought. *What have I done to this sweet old man? He probably threw it over his shoulder last time, and he wanted to show me what a big man he is.*

At the end of an hour, he looked at me and said, "You got anything stronger?" Because nothing had happened, obviously. Then he said, "This was known in the Kulu Valley long ago, but most yogis have forgotten it."

On later questioning, he said, "Well it could be useful, in a cool place, where you are feeling much peace, and your mind is turned toward God, and when you're alone." He said that it would allow you to come in and pranam, or bow to Christ, but you could only stay for two hours, and then you would have to leave again. He said, "You know, it would be much better to become Christ than to just visit with him. But your medicine won't do that, because it's a false samadhi"—which was exactly what Meher Baba had said to me. "Though," he said, "it's useful to visit a saint; it strengthens your faith." Then he added, "But love is a stronger medicine."

After that, once each year or two I would take LSD when I was peaceful and was alone and my mind was turned toward God, to sort of find out what was happening, and each time was profound in some way. With time, however, the relevance of psychedelics has diminished in my life to the point where I have no great desire to experiment further, though at times I still do it to see if I forgot anything.

For those who don't know about other levels of reality, LSD could, under proper conditions—where they feel safe and are truly turned toward spiritual life—show them that possibility. It did so for me. Once they know of the possibility and really want to get on with it, the game is not just to get high again but to "be," and *be* includes high *and* low. It is also true that now the culture has shifted and different kinds of realities are more accepted in everyday life. Many young people who never took acid and never smoked grass float in and out of planes; perhaps that's partly because of music, partly a result of the cultural shift that emerged from their parents' use of acid in the sixties. Don't underestimate the social changes that occurred as a result of psychedelics.

I don't deem that, for a being on the spiritual path, the LSD experience is necessary any longer. It is very clearly not a full sadhana; it won't liberate us. Because there is a subtle way in which there is attachment, in the sense of feeding our unworthiness because we aren't it without it, and we have to look outside ourselves to get hold of it. As a method, it also has the limitation that it temporarily overrides stuff that we would best deal with. Grabbing at experiences and pushing aside old habit patterns in order to get high is just delaying the process, because ultimately we have to confront those habit patterns and purify them.

After we know of the possibility, we get on with it, and any time we're just after another experience, we're just getting more hooked on experiences, and all experiences are traps. The game is to use a method, and then, when we're finished with it, to let it go. This isn't a good and evil matter; it's just a question of honesty with ourselves as to whether in fact we are using our opportunities as effectively as we can in order to awaken.

Because of the rampant use of opiates, cocaine, amphetamines, and prescription pain-killers, our society is running scared about all chemicals that alter consciousness. It's too bad that psychedelic (mind-manifesting) chemicals are being grouped together with the opium derivatives and other drugs that are primarily used for pleasure or escape. Psychedelic chemicals such as psilocybin, peyote, mescaline, LSD–25, DMT, MDA, and other tryptamines could play a profoundly beneficial role therapeutically and spiritually in our society if we approached their use with educated discrimination instead of categorizing them as illegal, ergo "bad." Because of their illegal status, there is a certain amount of paranoia associated with their use. If people are going to experiment, they must keep this in mind as something which affects their mind-set.

There is probably an appropriate stage in life to consider the use of psychedelics as a spiritual practice. It seems to be most disruptive for younger people who are still in the process of ego development—of becoming "somebody." On the other hand, there is potential spiritual value from this method for those who have developed good ground—i.e., they have their psychological, economic, and social act together on the physical plane—and who are able to create a supportive setting for this work in the kind of context Maharaj-ji suggested.

How do you open your heart?

A good exercise is to do deep breathing in and out of the heart as though it had nostrils, right in and out of the heart. You can use that breath to ferret out those places in you where there is a deep sadness or some deep attachments that are slowing your progress. Let them come forth and let them go; give them up to Kali or Christ or Guru or God. Keep bringing them out—the sadnesses deep within your heart that have closed you off—keep bringing them forward, keep going in and in until you're all the way back to your spine. Keep allowing the breath to more deeply fill this area, and then breathe it all out again.

Another way is to go out into the woods or to the ocean and with concentration make the gestures of opening the heart space, like Hanuman does when he tears open his chest to show Rām and Sita residing in his heart. We open the heart with breath or thoughts, and we call upon whomever we're in close contact with as a spiritual guide, perhaps Christ. We might say, "Christ, let me feel your love." We're not asking him to love us; we're asking to be allowed to feel the love he has for us. If we really open ourselves and ask that in truth, we can possibly feel a warmth starting to touch us, which will permeate us and start a process of our opening. Or we can sit with a picture of a being like Christ and just experience that love flowing back and forth between us and the picture.

It is just so incredibly gentle and beautiful starting a dialogue of love with a being who *is* love. Some of us have known Meher Baba, who is such great love, or Christ, who is a statement of love, who is love itself. We just open ourselves. We sit in a little meditation area with a picture of a being whose love is pure, whose love is in the light of God. It's not the love of personality, it's not the love of romance, it's not the needful love, "I need you." Romantic love is jealous and possessive because the object of that relationship becomes our connection to that place in us that is love. The kind of love that Christ gives is conscious, unconditional love; he just is love. And ultimately we become that kind of love. Then we're living in that space, and we don't need anybody to turn us on to love because we are it, and everybody who comes near us drinks of it.

And as we become more and more the statement of love, we fall in love with everyone. When we feel love when we are with each other, that opens us to the place in ourselves that is love. Sometimes when we feel that, we want to cling to each other because it's a love connection. But what we find is that we don't stay open to that place by collecting our connections; the only way to do it is to become love ourselves. Otherwise we're always going to be looking for connections. Most people want a Guru because they want a lover or a father. In fact, the Guru can be the guide to the beyond. Don't listen to what other people say about the Guru, or even what the Guru says about the Guru; we must listen to what our hearts say about the Guru.

If we follow our heart, there is nothing to fear. As long as our actions are based on our pure seeking for God, we are safe. And any time we are unsure or frightened about our situation, there's a beautiful and very powerful mantra—"The power of God is within me. The grace of God surrounds me"—which we can repeat to ourselves. It will protect us. Grace will surround us like a gentle force field. Through an open heart, one hears the universe.

How do you interpret statements like, "No man comes to the Father except through me"?

In almost all holy books, and especially in the words of holy beings, we are dealing with transmissions to different levels of disciples and devotees who can hear different things. Who was Jesus talking to? Are these the words of Jesus or of the Christ? We have really at least two beings in that one being. One of them is Jesus, who is the Son, a form of the Father made manifest on earth: "I am in the Father; the Father is in me."

Then there is the Christ, which is the consciousness out of which that form is manifested, the consciousness that acknowledges the Living Spirit. That's not necessarily Jesus, the man. The predicament is that, depending upon our degree of readiness, we become involved with the devotional relationship either to Jesus, the man, or to Christ, the consciousness, unconditional love. My experience of that particular biblical quote is that it is Christ speaking, not Jesus; that Jesus is a historical statement of the perfection made manifest, and at that historical moment, Christ said to somebody, "You can only come to the Father through me," though it may have been interpreted as coming from that body, which was Jesus. For someone else, at another moment, it means the greater body out of which that body comes, which is the Christ body. And that Christ consciousness is what would be called the Living Spirit. It's like the statement, "Eat of my flesh; drink of my blood." He didn't expect people to come up and tear off his arms or drink out of his veins; that is the universal form speaking, saying, "Consume the universe into yourself; drink of the universe so that you may know the Father." That's not Jesus speaking; that's the Christ.

The problem is that so much violence has been done by interpreting that initial statement as a statement of Jesus rather than as a statement of the Christ. Its misinterpretation has led to proselytizing, and a lack of acknowledgment of other people's ways of meeting the Christ other than through the form of Jesus.

A standard criticism not only of spiritual practice but of all forms of religion is that it's an opiate of the masses, it's a way of escape, it's a tool of the ruling class to take people's minds off of the social struggle and put it on some pie in the sky that they think will solve their problems, but won't really. What about it?

That's a very complex issue. In one sense they're absolutely right, in that when we enter into these other realities, the social/psychological/economic preoccupations and hardships look entirely different. I have met beings who live in conditions that I would consider subhuman, who are totally radiant, luminous, fulfilled, happy beings. Nobody's exploiting them; this is the way they *are*. They have choices, but it just doesn't matter to them. I look at them, and I don't see somebody who is drugged in the sense of "the opiate of the masses." I don't see somebody who has lost their freedom. That being has found something that makes worldly concerns less relevant to them. That doesn't make them bad or good, or weaker or stronger.

However, if spiritual seeking is used by one group of people to control another, that's another matter. Nobody has the right to control the consciousness of another human being. That applies to revolutionaries as well as to the establishment, and if I choose to sit quietly and be totally fulfilled in a room with no furniture, living on bread and water, I don't think I have to define myself as underprivileged or as suffering because I live below the standard of living. If somebody laid it on me against my will, that's oppression; but if I chose it as a means to extricate myself from deep conditioning, that's my business. Don't let paranoia rule the game about who's doing what to whom.

I believe in external *and* internal freedom, and I won't surrender my internal freedom for external freedom. Most Western activists want freedoms they can see and measure, the external freedoms. But somebody who is seeing clearly, I think, can recognize that even when we get all the external freedoms, which many people in the society actually have, we are still not free. That's what spirituality addresses itself to, the matter of inner, or internal freedom. Once we have internal freedom, we may or may not be political activists; we may or may not be artists; we may or may not be anything. Most likely, we won't sit around apathetically. But there isn't any rule that says we can't. That's external freedom. To say that everybody who is more conscious must be politically active is naïve, as far as I'm concerned, because a society is an extremely complex and exquisite organism, and it takes all kinds of parts to make it beautiful.

I see the evolutionary political change as very exciting, like a Martian takeover, rather than everyone picking up a gun and starting to shoot each other. It doesn't have to be "us" against "them." It's we become them, and then "them" becomes us. But it's scary, because there are no symbols to hide behind. Some who come and hang out with me are lawyers, doctors, and college professors. I don't say to them, "Give up being a doctor." I don't tell an activist to stop being an activist, or a politician to stop being a politician, or a singer to stop singing. We just do whatever we're doing in a way that increases the connection of humanity, the awareness of the interrelatedness of all things. That includes ecological sophistication, and economic and political awareness. Stay doing what you're doing, because there's no one role that defines the game. Just because you march on City Hall doesn't make you an effective political activist. Christ and Buddha were both effective political activists, each in his own way. I think we have to acknowledge that there are a variety of strategies in this game of life. And it isn't good guys and bad guys—it's just individual difference.

For those people who find themselves in a particular time and place in which it is appropriate for them to struggle politically against oppression and injustice, could spiritual practices help them?

Yes, because in terms of the effectiveness of any action, we are more effective when we are capable of being totally involved in what we're doing and totally non-attached—though I understand how the term *non-attached* might seem antagonistic to the original concerns that have motivated the involvement. Let me elucidate. Part of the total coolness that is needed when under stress comes from compassion for the entire predicament. That is, from having an overview of the whole game board. It's like fighting a ground battle, but you have the additional perspective of a helicopter overhead, studying the entire strategy. It allows us not to get so lost in our emotions that we make the other guy have to stay polarized. In other words, we give space for him to grow by seeing how he got caught in his predicament.

For instance, I can understand the position of, say, the Secretary of Defense, though I don't agree with it. I can protest his actions and say he shouldn't have done certain things, which I do. But at the same moment, I can hear his predicament. And that ability to hear his predicament gives him an opportunity to grow, because every human being has the right to get unstuck from his models. But the minute we take away people's opportunity to grow, even if they're bad guys, we've imposed on them exactly the wrongs we'd like to right. We can't create polarization in our zeal to override the bad guys, or we might create more.

As was said in *Be Here Now*, the hippies were creating the police, and the police were creating the hippies; it was so obvious in the Haight-Ashbury. The citizens got frightened by the scene, so they demanded their police get more oppressive. The police got more oppressive, and that became a symbol against which the hippies mobilized to fight. The more the hippies mobilized to fight, the more the police got oppressive. Each force was creating the other. And nobody in that space was conscious enough to cut through that polarization, which could have turned it into a whole collaborative dance together. I think that spiritual awareness, compassion, and consciousness can clearly contribute to political effectiveness.

You know Allen Ginsberg was incredible at the 1968 Democratic National Convention in Chicago. He just went and chanted OM right in the middle of the scene. Now that's a very interesting mixed game. At the time, I was sitting in a temple in India. I read some clippings about Allen in Chicago. And I went through a few changes, like, "Am I copping out? I mean, here's my buddy right there being maced and beaten. What am I doing? I'm sitting in a temple in the Himalayas in this room huddled in a blanket and making tea for myself. Is this a cop-out, or am I confronting other subtle demons for all of us, which in a way is as difficult as the demons, the bad guys, of the external physical plane? What can I bring to my fellow man?"

And it turns out that I do have something to offer political activists, or perhaps anyone who might share these words. It seems that a lot of revolutionary tactics in this country have won the battle but lost the war. If we alleviate human suffering on one level but our act doesn't allow it to be alleviated at another level, then we haven't accomplished the goal of ending suffering. Like in getting economic benefits for people, if we deepen their attachment to thinking that economic benefits are going to give them total peace or happiness, then we are perpetuating the illusion that causes the suffering. That's why the nature of the consciousness of the revolutionary determines whether the revolution ultimately liberates or entraps those it was meant to aid. It's a really beautiful issue. Really it's like the Europeans who originally came to America and thought that if they got political and religious freedom, they would have it made. Well, they came here and they got it, and they didn't have it made.

How does one decide to get rid of sexual desires? I'd like to give them up, but I don't know how.

We have finally found out in America that there really is nothing wrong with sex. We don't have to be Victorian about it. We've gone from neurotic sex to reasonably healthy sex, and that's really good. And if we're living in the world, sex is a very beautiful part of existence. However, if we in truth want to realize God in this lifetime, then we start to direct our energies toward getting there. The predicament with sexuality is that no matter how nice our intentions are, the act itself is so powerful that it catches us in the gratification that comes from our separateness, the extreme of sensual gratification. And in that sense, it's reinforcing our separateness. We don't give up sex because it's bad or wrong—no guilt, nothing like that. What we don't do is *give up* sex. What we do is acknowledge how much we want God, and we turn our hearts and minds in that direction without sounding like we're coming on for Barnum & Bailey. We can't get into a struggle against it, because every time we're busy struggling against something, we're reinforcing its reality. The game is just to go into the reality where sex is, like rubbing sticks together to make a fire. We get to the point where we're already existing in that place we were having sex to get to.

At times couples have said to me, "What's happening? As we get more into spirituality, our sex life means less and less to us. Something's wrong. Isn't sex divine?" Yes, sex is divine, but the reasons for having sex were falling away. Later they could have sex without any opposition or drain on their inner work. High beings can have the most incredibly beautiful sex imaginable because their hearts are open, which most people having sex in this culture don't experience. The problem is that most high beings don't have any desire for orgasm because they are already sharing such intimacy.

Tantra yoga is often played with by people who desire sexual gratification. They try to have their cake and eat it too. But in truth, when we desire to have a sexual relationship with another person, the arousal process and the gratification are reinforcing that desire. The only kind of truly Tantric sexuality that is possible is between two human beings who are so rooted in God that there is no preoccupying desire for the other person as "other." Then we may use the physiological process of body interaction in order to awaken energy to move it up through the chakras. But that is only when there is no preoccupying desire whatsoever in either partner. And that is a condition that hardly anybody I've ever known could fulfill. Short of that, let's just be honest with ourselves: sexuality is sexuality, not Tantra. The true Tantra is basically the relationship between Radha and Krishna, between the seeker and the Mother, where you open your soul and become both the lingam and the yoni, both the phallus and the vagina. You are both entering into the universe and drawing spirit into yourself—because the soul is neither male nor female. And when you have identified yourself as an awakening soul, the sexual dance starts to lose its pull.

But now I must caution you on what I'm saying. Each of us is at a different stage in our evolutionary cycle. Many of us have much work to do in interpersonal relations, sexual gratification and so on. That is the stage where we want to want God, but we have other business to attend to first. To make believe we are done with something we are not done with will slow us down in our spiritual journey. To try to hold on to something we are done with will equally slow our journey. There is no simple rule of the game of who becomes Brahmacharya and who doesn't. Some people do it, and some don't. Married couples may be Brahmacharya, or they may not. Brahmacharya couples have sex in order to produce a child, and that's it—not once a month on the new moon or by any formula.

We don't discard our sexuality. It's all part of the dance. And just like ultimately we can eat whatever we want, ultimately we can do whatever we want. This isn't a moral issue at all. If we can hear and be honest with ourselves, we'll know when we are done and when we are not done, and when one desire system is stronger than another. We just have to be straight with ourselves. Don't make believe. Phoniness is the worst part of spiritual life—people trying to be something they're not.

While some folks I encourage to be Brahmacharya, others I encourage to have sex. There are many horny celibates in this world who are not going anywhere except to psychiatrists. And there are a lot of people having sex who wish they weren't anymore but can't stop because they think they ought to be.

They've already entered into planes of consciousness where it's irrelevant. Trust yourself; allow your desires to fall away when it's appropriate.

What part does diet play in spiritual work?

As I hear it about diet, at different stages of our sadhana, different diets are indicated. We start to be pulled toward them. These are not based on morality. They are based on what vibratory rates we can ingest and transmute. And there are stages where we can't handle meat because of the vibratory rate, the rajasic, active quality of it, the hot intense passion of the stuff. We can't get calm enough through it. So our diet starts to lighten up, to fish and eggs, and vegetables and grains, dairy products and fruit. When we can't handle that, pretty soon we might get down to grains and dairy products, vegetables and fruit. Then there are times when we can't handle anything but fruit. And then we may go through a stage where we are so connected and clear and beyond it that we can eat anything again.

Certain diets will help purify the system when it's full of toxins from the kind of stuff we usually eat. They're really generally useful. Simple vegetarian diets often help. But don't get into a good-and-evil trip about it. It doesn't work. It's just getting caught in a lot of righteous morality. A lot of people are more preoccupied with what goes in their mouth than what comes out of it. I must honestly tell you that people have been liberated eating anything, so the game is clearly not going to be that simple. The Native Americans consumed buffalo, and there have been some very high mystics and saints among them. The Tibetans eat meat and honor the animals, and it is all part of the karmic working-through for all of them. And the way they do it is not spoiling or wasteful or angry or anything. It is in the way of things.

I remember meditating in Big Sur in a house that was loaned to me by Esalen Institute, and it came with a cat. Every morning the cat would go out and get its prey to eat. And it would come in, and because it loved me, it would come over to me and sit between my legs as I meditated. There, it would chew on the skull of a mouse or a lizard, which would sometimes still be alive and flapping. And I wouldn't know who to hate or who to love, or what to do. I learned a great deal. I was taken through a tremendous understanding of one level of our existence.

My diet has recently been modified vegetarian; that is, I eat fish and eggs, and now and then chicken. And I do that because it feels like my body needs a certain kind of protein, which I have to feed it because of my lifestyle. Just as I do, you too must listen to your own needs.

As a woman psychotherapist, I'm having a difficult time integrating what you teach with my daily work with my patients. Could you reflect a bit on this condition?

I think that the polarization of inner work and outer social action is a polarity that merely comes out of an attachment to a model in one's head. From my point of view, both of those come together very much in Karma Yoga, the yoga of daily life: Perform the daily actions of your life so as to come to a clearer state of consciousness or deeper peace or greater enlightenment or whatever metaphor you wish to use. The work you're doing becomes your practice rather than your practice taking you away from your daily life. That is, if you just start from where you are, not where you wish you were, and your givens are certain trainings and skills and responsibilities, then the game is to find within all that the path to enlightenment and the way to use it all as a method of working on yourself.

I find myself spending almost all of my time serving, being available to people who are suffering in one way or another. It's hard to define who's suffering how, or who's suffering more than another. When people come to me, my interaction with them is from their point of view allowing them to re-perceive their life strategies and their emotions and so on, but really they are my work on myself, just as arduous psychiatric patients are a psychiatrist's work on herself or himself. If you get lost in pity or anger or rejection or desire—sexual desire or desire for power over your patients—then you become less effective as an agent of change. Part of your work is to deal with countertransference and your own emotional reactions to people.

From my point of view, my work is to stay in a place of total involvement in the psychological plane with total nonattachment. I do what I do, and I do it as perfectly as my consciousness allows it to be done, though I'm not attached to how it comes out. I'm just doing it as best I can. It comes out as God wants it to come out, not as I think it ought to come out. That is, when I meet people, I don't immediately know if they ought to change just because they are in a mental hospital. I have no reason to say that how I think they ought to be is better than how they are. I just share my being with other beings, and they change to the extent they are capable and ready and can change, using my consciousness as an instrument.

Your struggle happens because a model of being a psychiatrist or being a woman or being any label is entrapping, because labels are limiting. They are finite; they have suffering connected with them. And part of the work of consciousness is to redefine your own being, your own nature, to the point where you *are*. Then there's psychiatristness and there's womanness and there's personalityness and there's opportunityness and so on. These are like phenomenal rings around your essence rather than who, at center, you really are. As long as you think you're somebody who's doing something, you're lost in the illusion and can't really offer anyone else the space to extricate themselves from their negative realities.

Now, the optimal strategy in behavior change, with yourself and every other human being, is compassion. That means, as far as I understand it, the ability to see how it all is. As long as you have certain desires about how you think it ought to be, you can't hear how it is. As long as I want something, I can't really understand it, because much of what I can see is just my own projective system. You come to see every human being, including yourself, as an incarnation in a body or a personality, going through a certain life experience, which is functional. You allow the incarnation to be just the way it is at this moment, seeing even your own confusion and conflict and suffering as functional rather than as dysfunctional.

The greatest thing you can do for any other being is to provide the unconditional love that comes from making contact with that place in them that is beyond conditions, which is just pure consciousness, pure essence. That is, once we acknowledge each other as existing, just being here, just being, then each of us is free to change optimally. If I can just love you because here we are, then you are free to grow as you need to grow, because none of it's going to change my feeling of love.

We're used to having these special-role relationships, thinking certain roles apply to one yet not to another, because we're very attached to externals—do you touch somebody, do you sleep with them, do you beat them, do you control them, do you collaborate with them, do you support them, do you pay them, do they pay you? That's all stuff of the interaction between two beings; it isn't the essence of the matter. As you work on yourself through your daily life, more and more you see your own reactions to things around you as sort of mechanical rip-offs. You get much calmer in the space behind it all, and you're able to hear more how it all is, including your own personality as a part of nature. The deeper you are in that space, the more there is available for everybody you meet who is capable of coming into that space. You are the environment that allows them to do that. And from within this space, all change is possible. The minute you identify yourself or anyone else with models, roles, or any characteristic, any individual difference, change is really fierce. When you live in a universe where you experience even your living and dying as relative rather than in absolute terms, it's all free to change. There's nowhere you have to go to work on yourself other than where you are at this moment, and everything that's happening to you is part of your work on yourself.

Different ones of us are different parts of the corpus of civilization, and no one act is any better than any other. If you didn't have the shoemaker, we would go unshod; you need the shoemaker. Is the shoemaker better than the psychiatrist or worse? And what about the garbage collector? Without garbage collection, you know where New York would be? Or Boston? So is the garbage man more important than the psychiatrist or less important? The whole thing becomes absurd. You begin to see that everybody, even the President, is just another instrument in the dance, another part of the total body, and each of us must hear what our particular route through is and not try to define, "That's a good one and the others are bad," or "That's the best one," or "I'm doing the most important work." The most important work you can do is the perfect job for *you* to do. Discover how to serve people not out of the fact that you're supposed to or *ought* to. Just do psychotherapy because that's where you're at. Do therapy as long as you realize that here we are behind doctorness and patientness; here we are behind neurosis and relative neurosis.

A very lovely psychiatrist I know is also interested in meditation and the spirit. It's remarkable, because his teacher is a black seventy-ish automobile mechanic who, from eight in the morning until six at night, works on cars and then comes home to his apartment, sits and drinks wine, and all these kids come and hang out around him because he's a wise man. And he heals them. He works on their bodies, but all the time he's transmitting this incredible unconditional love because he's loving the place in them behind all their crap and all the stuff and all the divine dance. And here's a psychiatrist who's willing to sit at the feet of this automobile mechanic because he's knowledgeable enough to respect wisdom.

I have three major instructions for my life from my Guru: love, serve, and remember. Love everyone, serve or feed everyone, and remember God. My own yoga seems to be doing every day whatever it is that I do—being with people, sharing time with them in whatever way. I don't demand they call themselves patients.

We may meet under any circumstances, in a restaurant or some-where, maybe a bus, and be with one another in whatever way we need to be with one another. In all cases it's my work on myself, because I am loving, serving, and remembering, but what I love and serve is a function of what I remember. What I remember is who we all are. I remember the Self—and that remembering means that my love and service toward another being are directed toward the place in them in which they are already free.

A few years ago, I used to meditate and I felt wonderful. Then my life changed, and now I look back and wonder what happened to that beautiful state of mind I had.

One difficulty most of us have is interpreting our suffering, and our doubt, and our confusion, and our loss of faith as part of the process of awakening. We keep feeling we fell out of grace—we blew it. "Why aren't I high? What happened? Life stinks. Before, it used to be all sweetness and light, and now it's so heavy for me." Not for all of us at all moments, but every one of us has those moments. I sure do.

It's like when Christ comes forth and performs all these miracles and says, "Look, it isn't the way you think it is at all. You aren't who you think you are; I'm not who you think I am. We are all in the Father. Come on, wake up. Let go of all your worldly nonsense. Let's get on with it." And everybody around him gets hooked on him because he's got all this power. Then he leaves them, and everybody gets depressed. They got hooked on their method, their method of getting high, and their method left. If you're a druggie, you ran out of drugs. Or, for me, my Guru left his body. Or a method that's been getting you high for years—singing to Krishna or following your breath—suddenly turns to straw in your mouth. It doesn't work anymore. What about all those lows? When you're angry. When you're getting fired. When you've run out of welfare. When your car breaks down. When there's an unexpected pregnancy. When there is a fight. When there is violence in the neighborhood. When there is racial tension in the community. When there is ecological disaster imminent at every turn. When there is a positive AIDS test. When politics all sound like lies.

All of this does an interesting thing: it throws us back in upon ourselves for us to see where we're at. When all the pins get pulled away, we have a chance for a moment to see what resources we have. There are many stages on this path, many lessons, but don't stop anywhere. It's all part of the process of awakening. You have all the time in the world, but don't waste a moment.

What is the Seva Foundation, which you helped form and are part of?

The word *seva* in Sanskrit means "selfless service." The Seva Foundation came into being in 1978 out of the inspiration of folks who served together in Southeast Asia as part of a World Health Organization (WHO) campaign that successfully eradicated smallpox from the face of the earth. SEVA was originally an acronym for "Society for Epidemiology and Voluntary Assistance."

Seva's first project was to help reduce the burden of preventable and curable blindness in the world. Eighty percent of third-world blindness can be prevented or cured. Nepal, the small, rugged country nestled in the Himalayas between China and

India, was the place Seva began work. Here was a situation in which Western know-how could really help. Seva undertook to help rid Nepal of its backlog of curable blindness and to develop an infrastructure that would enable Nepalis to become self-sufficient in eye care.

Seva collaborated in a Nepal Blindness Program by providing planning, expertise, administrators, assistance from ophthalmologists, medical supplies, vehicles, and support for training of the medical personnel. The program was directed at preventing potentially blinding diseases like trachoma, xerophthalmia, and keratomalacia through treatment and health education, and at reducing cataracts through surgeries via a network of hospitals, clinics, eye camps, and outreach programs.

Seva also collaborated with Aravind Eye Hospital, an extraordinary institution in Madurai, South India, that became a major source of inspiration for the work in Nepal. Its founder and a Seva board member, the late Dr. G. Venkataswamy, grew it from a twenty-bed clinic to a group of cutting-edge eye hospitals in South India that are a worldwide model for eye care. They do more cataract operations than any other institution in the world, and many Western ophthalmologists go there for internships. Seva also supports Aravind's initiatives in child health and nutrition, which reach the poorest of the poor in Indian villages.

Once the Nepal project was in place and work with Aravind was progressing, Seva broadened its mandate to relieve other kinds of suffering. They have worked with native peoples in Guatemala and Tibet and on Native American reservations in the Dakotas. Besides medical projects Seva works to enable indigenous cultures to carry on ancient crafts like weaving and traditional agriculture to support themselves. They also initiated a series of small reforestation projects in Africa, South America, Nepal, and South Dakota. A sister organization, Seva Service Society, was incorporated in Canada in 1982.

Behind the projects lies a vision that impels Seva to responsible actions that help to relieve suffering wherever possible; to create opportunities to grow spiritually and consciously through collaboratively cultivating the compassion of our own hearts; to acknowledge the earth as our home and our family; and to recognize that many of the problems facing humanity—hunger, poverty, physical suffering, fear and violence—can be reduced through dedicated human effort and helping people to help themselves. From the beginning Seva has valued a rapprochement on conscious action between social activists and spiritual seekers, the "do-ers" and the "be-ers." Largely a grassroots organization, Seva appreciates the wisdom of Gandhi's statement, "Whatever you do may seem insignificant, but it is most important that you do it". As an institution they are helping to ring the bell of compassion and joy in a sometimes bleak world, believing it's possible to do good and to have fun doing it, to open our love to God's love through an understanding that each of us works for all of us.

You can get more information at http://www.seva.org.

Who do you think you are? How do you view your role in the contemporary scene? How do you relate to it?

The most honest answer is, I have absolutely no idea who I am. I am not even fascinated anymore with who I am. I used to be fascinated with Ram Dass . . . "Wow, look at that. Isn't that interesting?" I try to get a rush off it now and then, but it's just not happening. Once John Lennon and Yoko Ono came to visit me. And a few days later so did Governor Jerry Brown. The old mind thought, *My God, a governor has come to my motel room. I must be somebody.* And I tried to get a little leverage off it, but it was empty—it was just nothing. I'm an old power tripper, so why wasn't I getting rushes off power?

I can speak to your question, and we can play this thing out. But most of the time, I'm just sitting pretty empty. It's quite incredible. It's the consciousness of other beings that draws all this stuff out of me. When I'm with you and you ask me who I am, I can give you a nice erudite answer. I might say I'm trained to be a wise man in this society. And I think that's a role that the society sure as hell can use.

My Guru said to me, "Lincoln was a good president because he knew that Christ was president and that he was only acting president." I don't really have any personal identity, except when I'm busy getting in the way. I don't think it's me doing this work. Sometimes I'm like a perfect instrument in a way, an instrument for the flow of the universe. I can't think of anything nicer than to be an instrument for the flow of the universe. I'm perfectly happy to be a pebble on the bottom of the lake. That's what's fun about having fame when you don't particularly want it. There's a freedom, not an entrapment, in it. There isn't much anxiety in my game anymore, because I'm just as interested in it whichever way it goes.

In the sixties I was really a bad guy in this society, an acid head thrown out of Harvard and all that. Now I'm a good guy in the society. Maybe I'll be a bad guy in the society again someday. It's just the flow, just the dance. I just notice it.

All I really want to do is become free. And more and more, no matter what I'm doing, that's all I'm doing anyway. I'm sitting here, and it's just going through me. It's just nothing. It's totally beautiful, and the more nothing it is, the more beautiful it gets.

All of the things I would share with you are unspeakable. It is only now that we have this book out of the way that we can start to dance into the realms where we look into one another's eyes and know what is not know-able. We are that, for ultimately we will transcend knowing. And we will be wise—a simplicity out of which comes the wisdom of our being. A human birth is a very precious matter. We have all the ingredients necessary to know God fully in this lifetime. That we all reached forth to meet here is itself incredible grace.

"Rejoice in the Lord always. And again I say, rejoice.
Rejoice, rejoice, and again I say rejoice."